PRAISE FOR *IS IT JUST ME?*

"Grace Valentine doesn't merely ask a question: *Is It Just Me?* She's offering an unchanging solution when we need it most—right now!—when things aren't okay, when it's hard to trust God. This book will bring you hope in the dark. I honestly don't know of a voice more life-giving or a heart more Jesus-clinging to guide us than Grace Valentine."

—RASHAWN COPELAND
AUTHOR OF *START WHERE YOU ARE*
INSTAGRAM: @HYPESIR

"Grace has done it again! *Is It Just Me?* is a phenomenal read that will speak to the hearts of both students and adults. This book consists of five incredible parts that are inspirational, motivational, and life-giving! Grace speaks directly to individuals who have dealt with the feelings of hurts, doubts, or trying to find your purpose. It's a book that reminds us all that we don't have to be perfect; we have to trust and believe in our heavenly Father, who is perfect and loves you unconditionally! In a time of great uncertainty and ambiguity, I genuinely believe this is one of those books that is a *must read*! It will help you strengthen your faith and remind you that you've been redeemed."

—JEFF WALLACE
EXECUTIVE DIRECTOR OF YPS AND LIFT TOUR
AT STUDENT LEADERSHIP UNIVERSITY

"Talk about a breath of fresh air. Grace Valentine takes the pressure off of being perfect from page one until the final word of *Is it Just Me?*—and in the process, that stunning relatability points us to the only answer, the only Savior, and the only One who is truly enough. I love this sister, and I love this book."

—LISA WHITTLE
BESTSELLING AUTHOR OF *JESUS OVER EVERYTHING*,
PODCAST HOST, AND BIBLE TEACHER
@LISAWHITTLE

"After reading this book, you feel like Grace Valentine is your new best friend. Her heart jumps off the pages, and her relatability will resonate with every reader. A good book always feels like a conversation between the author and the reader, and that's how *Is It Just Me?* made me feel. It is so amazing to see Grace allow the Lord to use her platform to bring light and truth to those struggling or in need of advice all over the world."

—KENNEDY STIDHAM
FASHION AND LIFESTYLE BLOGGER
@KENNEDYSTIDHAM

"I wish my daughter was best friends with Grace. Wow. This book is as real as it can get. It's transparent, bold, and in your face. For all of us living and fighting with insecurities, this book is gonna help you find you and rediscover who God made you to be."

—JOIVAN JIMÉNEZ
GMA DOVE AWARD-NOMINATED ARTIST AND
PASTOR AT MEADOWBROOK CHURCH
@JOIVANJIMENEZ

"*Is It Just Me?* is a book I will reread over and over again. I can't put it down! Grace has a way with words that makes others feel less alone in their journey. I read these pages feeling seen and understood by her stories and encouragement. *Is It Just Me?* addresses many real experiences with authenticity, honesty, and hope. I have no doubt that this book will be a healing tool for many readers to draw closer to God while being comforted by the reminder that they're not alone as they navigate their hurts, doubts, and fears."

—MADISON WHEAT
FOUNDER OF AND WRITER FOR @METOOSISTER

"One word continually comes to my mind while reading this book: authentic. In a society that's obsessed with perfection, we are left with feelings of inadequacy, anxiety, and loneliness. I celebrate Grace for sharing difficult real-life experiences, and I admire how she covers them in truth. I'm left encouraged to laugh at the impossible standard of perfection and to instead chase toward the freedom of being imperfectly in this together!"

—MAIA MAE BILLMAN
MM FOUNDER AND CEO OF MM DESIGNS,
A FAITH-BASED RETAIL COMPANY
@MMDESIGNS____

"This is the kind of book that not only brings healing but brings transformation to your soul if you let it. Grace Valentine speaks from a place of experience, which creates a space of relatability for us to be present in. Such an empowering read."

—HOPE MOQUIN
COLLEGE DIRECTOR AND AUTHOR
@HOPEMOQUIN

"Grace uses her God-given talent to unapologetically reveal her heart as she honestly and openly navigates her own relationship with Christ. *Is It Just Me?* is a love letter to each of us, inducing conviction and requiring an examination of our own hearts, with a promise of a God who yearns to know us."

—LAUREN O'CONNELL
CBS *SURVIVOR* FINALIST AND PHILANTHROPIST
@LAAUREN.ALEXANDRA

"Finally, a book filled with answers to honest questions! Grace Valentine very candidly lays open her private questions about her own life while sharing with the reader the answers she's found in Scripture. She writes with a truthful, honest edge that conveys the credibility of her experience as a young Christian woman. Grace's warm and inviting voice will make you feel like you are sitting across the table from her, sharing an experience while she lovingly listens, affirms, yet still manages to challenge you to push past the pain into healing found only in Jesus. This book will meet so many young women in a place of confusion and lead them out with the clarity provided in God's Word. Grace is a fresh and comforting voice for her generation and many to follow."

—ANGIE ELKINS
HOST, *CHATOLOGIE* PODCAST
@ANGIEBROWNELKINS

"Grace, in all her humor and honest glory, has a knack for making every girl feel as if she's not alone! The actionable steps she shares show that peace is indeed possible. Her words will invite you into the conversation and challenge you to show grace for not only others but yourself. Here's to overcoming struggles one page at a time."

—TARAH-LYNN SAINT-ELIEN
AUTHOR OF *CLAIM YOUR CROWN*, MISS BLACK NEW
JERSEY 2018, AND CREATOR OF @ADORNEDINARMOR

"Grace beautifully exposes our world of misconceptions and lies to empower readers to abide in the depths of God's truth and love. *Everyone* has something to learn by reading *Is It Just Me?*"

—LUKE BEAMER
WRITER OF @UNLABELEDWORD

"Grace is not afraid to share her real and relatable experiences to ensure the readers that they are not alone in the struggles they face and the questions they ask. I encourage anyone who needs to be reminded that Jesus is faithful through the good, bad, and ugly to read this book."

—MADDIE KITCHEN
CHRISTIAN BLOGGER
@MADDIEE_JOY

IS IT JUST ME?

Learning to Trust God in the Middle of Hurts, Doubts, and Fears

grace valentine

W PUBLISHING GROUP

AN IMPRINT OF THOMAS NELSON

Published in Nashville, Tennessee, by W Publishing, an imprint of Thomas Nelson.

The author is represented by MacGregor Literary, Inc.

Thomas Nelson titles may be purchased in bulk for educational, business, fundraising, or sales promotional use. For information, please e-mail SpecialMarkets@ThomasNelson.com.

ISBN 978-0-7852-3396-1 (eBook)

Library of Congress Control Number: 2020943223

ISBN 978-0-7852-3395-4

Printed in the United States of America

21 22 23 24 25 LSC 10 9 8 7 6 5 4 3 2 1

To my parents, brother, and grandmas.
Thank you for always having my back.
And also, to any girl reading this from
Mandeville, Louisiana, God's got big
plans for you. Dream the big dreams.

CONTENTS

INTRODUCTION

Just Me

Typically, in the beginning of a book like this, the author introduces herself and lists all her accomplishments. This is the place where you would read about her years of extensive seminary stud ies before she describes how she went to heaven and came back, met Oprah, or, perhaps, has been blessed by God with a hot spouse, four beautiful kids, and two golden retrievers with such *distinct personalities*. She tells you all this to gain your trust, to prove to you that she deserves to be an author.

Well, this is not that kind of book.

I wrote this book because I was tired of reading books written by "perfect" Christians. I searched the bookstore shelves for someone I could relate to. I wanted honesty. I wanted relatability. I wanted to believe I wasn't the only one dealing with crap. I wanted to stop thinking, *Is it just me?* So I wrote this book for regular girls like me who sometimes feel alone.

My name is Grace Valentine, and I'm simply a twentysomething author still figuring out life. I'm *far* from perfect. So let me begin this book by being really honest with you.

I live in a city where rent is too high, and I often live paycheck to paycheck. My mother is the greatest person I know, but she seems resigned to the belief that, at this point in my life, I'll never convince a guy to marry me. Or, frankly, even date me. I've eaten Chick-fil-A four times this week and haven't bought groceries in over two weeks. I went for a run today but started walking sooner than I'd like to admit. Oh—and I cried last week over a guy I haven't even dated.

Some could claim that I'm a mess, but I prefer to believe that I'm a work in progress. I mean, Rome wasn't built in a day, right?

When I was a college student, I spent most of my nights at frat parties. I said I believed in Jesus but lived a "Hannah Montana" Christian life: I wanted the best of both worlds. I wanted Jesus and heaven, but I also wanted to pursue my own desires. If you had told me freshman year that I would write Christian books, I would have laughed. Loud. But God had different plans.

I'm not the kind of person you would expect to write books about faith and life. Perhaps that's what makes God so cool—He uses people like you and me to bring Him glory. He uses our mistakes and mess-ups to make His name great. Even people like me can turn their lives around from doing shots and keg stands to writing books about Jesus.

All that confessed, why am I writing this book? Why do I believe my words carry value?

I don't know about you, but I just want to hear from people like me who struggle, mess up, and occasionally battle against insecurity but point me to the Bible and God's truth. I don't need "perfect" because if I've learned anything in my life so far, it's that behind every "perfect" role model is a sinner who still struggles. Instead of perfection, I want real. Instead of pretend, I want genuine.

Don't you want that too?

If so, welcome to this book—a book written by a struggling twentysomething who believes there should be more regular girls writing books.

From the start, you need to know some things about me. I smile big but also hide a lot. Life has been hectic for me lately. I'm learning a lot about how to handle my life, faith, and emotions when I'm overwhelmed and annoyed. The truth is that my life kind of feels like it's in the middle of season five, and the director is causing havoc in a semi-desperate attempt to keep things interesting. For the longest time, I thought I was alone in this feeling. Everyone else seemed happier, more successful, and like they had their lives together better than me. For the longest time, I couldn't help but think, *Is it just me?*

I wrote this book during one of the busiest seasons of my life. I was traveling to promote my first book, working a full-time ministry job, trying to maintain a decent social life, going on a few dates, and—most importantly—trying not to eat too many carbs. Life was overwhelming. Paying bills was scary. The future freaked me out. On some hard days, I doubted God even existed, let alone was good. And along the way, I was constantly frustrated by people, my circumstances, and the plain ol' everyday hustle. I felt alone.

During this season, I reflected on my many years of feeling inadequate and annoyed. College was great. And, at times, it kind of sucked. My past relationships with friends and guys had created trust issues, both minor and major. As I reflected, I realized that for way too long I had felt overwhelmed and all alone.

I felt stuck but at the same time I felt as if I was racing a million miles a second. I felt mediocre in the many avenues of my life. What was wrong with me? Was I the only one who felt this way?

Then one Tuesday when I was driving to work, probably pouting about something insignificant, I realized something important: I'm not alone. Watching the many cars around me also hustle to get somewhere reminded me this is a big world, and we all have big struggles.

Other people struggle too. However, we are struggling because we feel the pressure to please instead of the peace that comes from trusting Jesus. And when I trust in Jesus, I have a Savior who reminds me *it is not just me.* I have Him, and I have truth.

Now, here we are, ready to become friends through the pages of a book. I want you to know this: Yes, I have felt alone. But the truth is, I'm not alone. And neither are you. I am tired of a world that tells us women to smile and pretend to have our lives together. No, that is not what this book is about. In this book, we are going to wipe off our fake smiles and be honest about the issues, doubts, and fears we face. We are going to relate to one another.

Let this book become a journey for you—a journey where you stop feeling alone and realize two things:

1. *We all have issues.* We all have burdens. We all have days when we are weary and frustrated. You are not alone in your doubts and fears. You may have felt alone, but that isn't because your struggle is unique; it is because we have all told the "I'm fine" lie for far too long. Let this book allow you to become honest with yourself and those around you. Breakthrough begins when you break up with the lie that time heals all wounds. Wounds are healed when you acknowledge the scar and run to the ultimate Healer.

2. *You have a Savior who loves you and wants the real you.* We all have struggles, yes—but we all have a Savior. When you give Him true trust and learn how to lean on Him for strength, you can get through every single hard day. You can and will get through all the tears, failures, doubts, and mistakes. You are not alone because you have a Savior who right now is asking you, *Will you finally stop pushing Me away? Will you finally trust in Me?*

So I invite you to join me in the story of my journey—one of realizing I am not alone, finding my true trust in Jesus, and renewing my strength in Him. When I am struggling, nothing frustrates me more than someone telling me about all the things they are doing right. I promise to be honest with you. I will share my fears, doubts, and mistakes. And since I am not hiding behind any lies about who I am, I also want to challenge you to stop pretending. We are not going to "fake it till we make it" here. We are going to speak our truth and search for the truth that comes from our Savior. We will do this together—one train wreck to another.

Our Trust Issues

As we start our journey, I want you to write out this passage of Scripture and stick it on your bathroom wall or in your planner or make it your phone's screen saver—wherever it's visible to you:

> Even youths will become weak and tired,
>   and young men will fall in exhaustion.
> But those who trust in the Lord will find new strength.
>   They will soar high on wings like eagles.
> They will run and not grow weary.
>   They will walk and not faint.
>
> Isaiah 40:30–31 NLT

God is not surprised that we get tired and overwhelmed. Here in Isaiah, we see this passage start off by saying, "Even youths will become weak and tired . . ." But if we trust in the Lord, as Isaiah assured us, we can receive renewed strength through Him.

The reason I felt so overwhelmed and alone in my struggles was that I was relying on my own strength. I believed all the lies that you might believe as well:

I've got this!

I can do this on my own!

And the old faithful, *I am all I need.*

For years, out of fear of rejection, I avoided trusting anyone, including God. I thought if I just handled my issues myself, my life would be okay. I kept huffing and puffing along the way only to come up short of where I thought I could get on my own.

I was weary because I was forgetting to do what this verse says: *trust in the Lord.*

During our journey, where together we will figure out how to deal with feeling all alone in our struggles, please do me this favor: let's work through our trust issues.

I think trust issues cause many of us to struggle to trust God to supply our strength on difficult and lonely days. We believe we have been failed by the church, Christians, friends, family, and, well, almost everyone else. We stopped trusting Jesus and claimed we were just being realistic.

That's one of the intriguing parts about faith—it was never meant to be realistic. Relying on a Spirit you cannot physically see to give you strength is not realistic. Soaring on wings like eagles when you have a nine-to-five job and kids waiting for you at home is not realistic. Soaring on wings like eagles while you're a college student being judged by people because of your past is not realistic. Learning to trust can feel impossible if you have been cheated on, had your heart broken, or been betrayed by a close friend. Growing in your faith is not realistic when you're busy in college and eating Taco Bell at 3:00 a.m. because midterms suck. But, my friend, believe me when I say it is possible to do all those things if we ditch our trust issues and cultivate a trust that is stronger than our weariness.

I don't have all the answers. What I do have, though, is peace. This peace didn't bibbidi-bobbidi-boo and appear to me one random night.

God is not like a fairy godmother we run to when we want a more peaceful life. There's no magic wand that He waves to make our lives instantly better. Instead, He gives us something more powerful and more fulfilling—He gives us Himself. And when I leaned in to Him for my strength, I discovered true trust.

Learning to Trust God Together

Too often we make Christianity sound as if it should bring instant transformation. And in a way, it does. When you believe in your heart and confess Jesus with your mouth, He immediately saves you (Romans 10:9). You are made new. But that does not mean life gets easier. Being a Christian doesn't mean you won't have bad days.

Here's the truth: true trust takes work. The reason I felt alone and couldn't walk in trust was that I was holding back on authenticity. My trust issues with Jesus and others were taking a toll on my emotional and physical health.

In this book we will explore some of the questions I struggled with:

- Am I the only one who is tired, overwhelmed, doubting, and fearful?
- Am I the only one who feels hurt and lonely?
- Am I the only one who is still searching for my purpose?
- Am I the only one struggling to trust that God is there?
- Am I the only one confused about how to be an adult?
- *Is it just me?*

If you are tired of feeling like it's just you, then buckle up! Together, I want us to look at our hurts, doubts, and fears and let God fill our hearts with true trust so that we can soar like eagles through this adventure we call life.

As you read, please be honest not only with yourself but also with God. Take time to answer the "Real Talk" prompts and pray after each chapter. Reflect on your past, and then ask God to reveal areas of growth for you. And always remember: it's not just you—and you are never alone. There is joy to be had, adventure to be lived, and laughter to be shared. Our lives are imperfect, yes, but together we can lean on one another and lean on our Savior. You can experience joy instead of loneliness and true trust instead of hurt . . . and I'm excited to be on this journey with you.

Real Talk

- Of the list of six questions above, which do you expect to relate to the most? Why?
- Name one struggle in which you feel all alone. Why does that struggle feel so isolating?
- Write a prayer asking God to show you areas in which you have trust issues with Him. Ask God to reveal the adventures He has for you in your everyday life.

Part 1

AM I THE ONLY ONE WHO IS TIRED, OVERWHELMED, DOUBTING, AND FEARFUL?

WHEN EXHAUSTION MEETS BURNOUT

I want it all. And by all, I mean a social life that excites me, family time that refreshes me, a job that I'm good at and makes me come alive, eight hours of sleep each night, a balanced diet, arms that can lift a decent weight, and a body that doesn't get winded every time I take the stairs.

Is that too much to ask?

Well, after twenty-three years of being burned out and tired, I found out that, yes, it was. It was impossible to have my dream life. There weren't enough hours in the day to have it all. Instead of eagerness and adventure and my perfect dream life, I carried exhaustion and a sense of frustration.

Why can't life just go my way? Why can't I control my life and create the life I want? Am I the only one who feels this way?

The truth is that we can control our lives. Of course, I am not saying that we are God; we are not the authors of our stories. We can't control our circumstances, but we can control our perspectives. Life is not about what happens to us; it's about how we respond and control our thoughts.

Three Steps to Avoid Burnout

I can't emphasize it enough: you aren't alone in your struggles. I have a feeling that as you read through the following three steps to avoid burnout, you'll see something that relates not only to you but also to those who have trusted you with their hurts, doubts, and fears. We are smiling through the hurt, but we are also burning ourselves out. So to start this journey, let's take these three steps.

Step 1. Identify your burnout.

If you don't recognize your weariness, you can't receive strength from God. You cannot experience true freedom without an awareness that you are stuck in bondage. For me, it took recognizing that my hustling, frustration, and weariness were flaws of my own thoughts before I could work toward and then receive freedom.

Step 2. Pause and find the cause.

What is the cause of your weariness? Weariness often comes when we chase the wrong things. Within this step, we will look at four common pursuits that cause us frustration and weariness. For each pursuit, I'll give you an opportunity to rate yourself on a scale of 1 to 10, with 1 being not a problem and 10 being a problem you face multiple times per day.

Pressure to Prove Yourself

The person who struggles in this area often wastes her time trying to convince others that she is worthy. She carries rejection from the past that makes it difficult for her to believe and trust that God's love is all she needs. She believes that labels and reputation hold more weight than Scripture. This person will forget a compliment after twenty-four hours yet cling to a negative word for years.

- Highlight or underline the phrase(s) in the preceding paragraph that you relate to most.
- On a scale of 1 to 10, how much do you struggle in this area?

6

Ask yourself these questions:

1. When was the last time you were rejected? How did you respond to the rejection?
2. Do you struggle to believe that God's love is more valuable than being well liked? Why or why not?
3. What was the last hurtful word or action you remember? What was the earliest one that you remember?

Addiction to Success

This person has tasted success and, despite its temporary nature, continually chases the addiction of success—whether through grades, a job, family life, or social life. This person often spends more time working than resting. Idle time frustrates her, and jealousy is her natural reaction. When others succeed, instead of being happy for them, she wonders how she could replicate their work ethic. Rest does not come easily for her, and she prioritizes her output over her input. Thus, she spends more time doing big things than receiving truth in small doses regularly.

- Highlight or underline the phrase(s) in the preceding paragraph that you relate to most.
- On a scale of 1 to 10, how much do you struggle in this area?

8

Ask yourself these questions:

1. In what area of your life do you hustle too much?
2. When you see someone succeed, what goes through your mind? Is there an example of a time when you remember becoming jealous?
3. Do you tend to prioritize your output more than your input? How has this affected your patience level at school, home, or work?

Desire to Make Others Feel Loved

This person spends more days thinking about others than herself. Although her empathy and compassion are well intended, she often ends up feeling empty. Burnout is common for this person, and even if outwardly she loves others well, inwardly she slowly becomes more overwhelmed and insecure. She is patient, but over time, she eventually releases her frustration on others. This person struggles to love herself and doesn't think highly of herself because she fears no one will show her love and reassurance in the manner she needs. Communicating vulnerability is difficult for her because she doesn't want to bother anyone. As a result, she struggles to feel the freedom to be who she truly is.

- Highlight or underline the phrase(s) in the preceding paragraph that you relate to most.
- On a scale of 1 to 10, how much do you struggle in this area?

5

Ask yourself these questions:

1. Do you feel like love has to be earned? Why or why not?
2. Have you ever loved someone well, only to have that person reject you? If so, how did this experience affect your perspective on life today?
3. Describe a time when you were vulnerable and got betrayed. Does this experience make it difficult for you to trust today?

The Yes Effect

Whether it's because bills need to be paid and her family has to be taken care of or she simply feels that if she doesn't step up, no one will, this person is tired because she keeps saying yes. She forgets that no is not a negative response. This person tends to struggle with physical weariness and, due to her physical weariness, easily becomes <u>frustrated</u> with people who don't move as quickly as she does. [She finds it difficult to empathize with others because her life is so busy.]

- Highlight or underline the phrase(s) in the preceding paragraph that you relate to most.
- On a scale of 1 to 10, how much do you struggle in this area?

5

Ask yourself these questions:

1. Do you feel the need to routinely say yes? Why or why not?
2. What are the pros and cons of saying yes?
3. How do the cons of saying yes affect your perspective of life?

Step 3. Seek truth.

You opened this book for a reason—perhaps because you have felt alone in your struggles for far too long. If you want to experience a sense of belonging, eagerness, and adventure, you must take a bold step closer to truth. Now, stepping toward the truth is not easy. But with each step toward truth, you are getting closer to the One who is with you and gives you joy during your difficult days. Together, we will seek truth.

The Next Step Toward Freedom

We all struggle with each of these areas at times. But here's the good news: we all can take the next step toward freedom and leave weariness in our rearview mirror. How do we do that? It requires truth.

Throughout this book you will have many opportunities to grow. But first, I want to ask you to do one last thing for now: *increase your ceiling.* What do I mean by that? If you want to grow, you have to increase your ceiling so you have room to bloom. Think of it this way: a flower's growth and height are dependent on its environment. If you move a flower outside toward the sunshine, where the sky's the limit, it can bloom larger and higher. The same is true with you.

As we begin to work together through our struggles, fears, and trust issues in this book, we need to plant ourselves in an environment where the sky is the limit. We do not want to be in a small, dark closet, stuck in a space where growth is limited. Instead, make room to bloom. This might require that you step into a new friendship, a new environment, or even a new desire for vulnerability. But start now and take the next step toward creating an environment that makes room for you to increase your possibilities.

Real Talk

- Of the four pursuits listed in this chapter that cause us frustration and weariness, which one do you tend to chase the most?
- Do you feel burned out? If so, in what area? Why?
- What is one way you can work toward creating an environment that helps you grow and increases your possibilities to find truth? If you are reading this as part of a group, what is one way that your group can help one another make room to bloom?

02

WHEN BUSYNESS BECOMES A BADGE

I returned home to New Orleans for my five-year high school class reunion. I know what you're thinking: *Who has five-year class reunions?* Our class did, and I had to plan the reunion because seventeen-year-old class president Grace Valentine promised she would. And who wants to be pointed at as the one who reneged on her promise?

I'd be lying if I said I wasn't nervous before the reunion. I had gained twenty pounds since high school, and my dress made me feel pudgy.

I was scared people would ask about my relationship status, and I'd have to sip on my Moscow Mule and force a smile while saying, "Still single!"

I was scared people would ask about my career and financial stability, and I'd have to confess that my Louis Vuitton is actually a

"Fooey Vuitton." My purse may look like it is worth two thousand dollars, but the truth is, it's a knockoff. And I was scared my peers would think *I* was a knockoff too.

I was scared of seeing people I had ended friendships with on a bad note and having to say something like, "Hi, I realize I didn't care about you enough to talk to you for the past five years, but now that I am here at this reunion alone, how are you?"

I knew I was being dramatic, but I couldn't help it.

During the reunion, a guy friend told me, "I'm surprised you still had time to throw this reunion! Aren't you so busy, Grace?"

Wow, he thought I was busy. What a strange honor! My ego grew as the words entered my ears.

"Yeah, I mean, I am *sooo* busy. Life has been crazy, but I'm glad to be here. I made time for this."

The way I described my busyness during the next couple of conversations with classmates could have made for a comedy movie. I bragged about my to-do list as if my busyness were a trophy. Every time someone asked how I was doing, I responded, "I'm doing so good! Just super busy! But good."

I was busy. But my ego caused me to praise the characteristics of my busyness that did not deserve praise. My busyness had become an idol. I was finding my worth in my productivity, not my purpose. I was finding my worth in my schedule, not my Creator.

I wrongly believed that my purpose was to be in motion, not to be with Christ.

What about you? Do you, too, sometimes take pride in how busy you are? We wear this badge of busyness because we feel defined by what we do. And when we feel defined by what we do, we ignore what Jesus has already done.

We tend to feel defined by our to-do lists when we think we are the only ones who are struggling in our current season. We are desperate to prove we have worth, so we exhaust ourselves with busyness. But every time we do that, we come up short because we are exhausting ourselves instead of trusting God.

So to you, my busy friend, let's throw off our badges of busyness because our worth can't be found there. Let's find truth in these three points.

Jesus Never Asked You to Be Busy

If you're anything like me, you say yes without thinking, and then you find yourself in over your head. Life keeps moving faster, and some mornings you wonder if there ever will be an eye cream good enough to hide your bags. I get it. However, Jesus never asked you to be busy.

Don't let your plans distract you from God's purpose for you. There's nothing wrong with keeping a calendar. There's nothing wrong with having plans. But a crucial question to ask yourself is, "Am I pursuing my plans or His purpose?"

Focusing on our will often distracts us from God's will. Too often our will is to be busy, be productive, and achieve success by the world's standards. But God's will is for us to sit at His feet, focus on Him, and pursue our relationship with Him. We will never know why we were created if we don't know our Creator and Savior.

Only One Thing Truly Matters

I get it. You want to do well. You want to do well in your job, your school, your family, and your social life. I do too. Those are not necessarily wrong pursuits. But if you feel overwhelmed by life's demands, it's probably because you lost sight of what life is all about. Only one thing truly matters.

I love a story from the Gospel of Luke in which Jesus was invited

home of a woman named Martha. Martha's sister, Mary, also
there, and they each handled Jesus' presence differently. Martha
as busy preparing dinner while Mary sat at Jesus' feet and listened
as He taught.

Martha came to Jesus and said it wasn't fair that she was so
busy while Mary did nothing to help. Martha even asked Jesus to
tell Mary to start helping. Jesus' reply must have shocked Martha:
"'Martha, Martha,' the Lord answered, 'you are worried and upset
about many things, but few things are needed—or indeed only one'"
(Luke 10:41–42).

Martha was more productive than her sister, but she was missing
out on her purpose. It's important to note that the work Martha was
doing was important. She was busy making dinner for her guests. But
the task that was keeping Martha busy wasn't holy. In fact, verse 40
says that when Jesus came into her home, Martha was "distracted by
all the preparations that had to be made."

The lesson from the story of Martha and Mary is this: you have
one purpose, and it is Jesus. Your purpose is to love Jesus. To be with
Jesus. To show Jesus to others.

People Are Impacted by You, Not Your Success

A lot of people today struggle with busyness. It's not just you! Others
are struggling too. And they need a purposeful you, not a busy you.
Now, I'm not saying don't do your work. Hustle like mad. Go to
work. Work your butt off. But if you want to make a difference in
this world, stop being too busy for God. And stop being too busy for
God's people.

Some of Jesus' most powerful moments recorded in the Bible
happened over dinner with outcasts. Don't get me wrong—Jesus
performed many miracles. And when Jesus went to the cross, that was

the single most important event that will ever take place in history. But what made people talk and caused crowds to follow Jesus was His ability to love those who had been rejected by others.

Jesus' actions confused the religious leaders of His day. Why would a busy rabbi take time to talk to sinners and outcasts? Think about all the things Jesus could have put on His to-do list during the three years He was ministering on earth. Yet the One who could do all things still thought it was important to spend time with others and share a conversation.

If you become too busy to be intentional, you probably aren't living out your purpose. You will miss out on big opportunities to love your big Savior when you're busy being busy. What a shame it would be if you and I missed out on our purpose because we were too busy!

When our busyness becomes a badge of honor that we proudly wear to find our worth, we create a shield that pushes away true friendships and ministry opportunities. People see your badge of busyness and think you're too busy for them, so they don't want to bother you with their hard day.

Do you see the cycle here? We find our worth in our busyness because we feel alone, and then in response, others become too scared to approach us, so they feel alone too. In this cycle, everyone is lonely, and no one is learning to trust in God. In this cycle, you miss out on opportunities to leave an impact on this world. Focus on changing the world, not trying to please the world.

Come as You Are

To my busy, overwhelmed, and tired friend, I encourage you to drop your worries. Drop your anxieties. Drop your to-do list. Drop your plans if they are getting in the way of your time with sweet Jesus. Your

...e is more than your job, your activities, your financial stability, ...our calendar.

Jesus doesn't want your schedule, your hustle, or your good deeds. He wants you.

When Jesus said, "Come to me, all you who are weary and burdened, and I will give you rest" (Matthew 11:28), He didn't say, "Hey, come when you have space in your life; I know that may not be till your next vacation day probably months from now." Instead, He was saying, "Come as you are." Jesus wants you to come right now, in your weariness, in your crazy work week, in the mess, and sit at His feet. He wants you to be authentically you and not try to impress Him with your to-do list and full résumé. He meant for you to come now. Even in the midst of your messy, busy life.

Maybe you're in college and feeling overwhelmed with school, or maybe you're a young adult feeling overwhelmed with adulting. Maybe you're a mom with young children or a single woman killing it at work. Whatever your situation, I encourage you to make time for Jesus.

Be with Jesus. Be with Jesus now. Call out to Him and give Him your silence so He has an opportunity to speak.

Open your Bible and read His Word. Take a few minutes to stop focusing on all your things, and choose instead to be still and focus on Him.

How are you supposed to figure out your purpose in life if you aren't doing your life with the One who created you? How are you supposed to change the world if you're not first sitting at the feet of the One who made the world?

Many people will tell you to hustle. Many will tell you that each day is about working harder and becoming smarter. But I promise you this, my friend: *you can work as hard as you want, but if you aren't sitting at the feet of Jesus, you're missing out on your true purpose.*

Go to work, study for the test, and do your squats. But first, sit quietly alone. Separate yourself from the hustle. Open your Bible, and talk to Jesus.

Jesus wants you, not your hectic life and hustle. Seek Him first so you won't miss out on His beautiful kingdom.

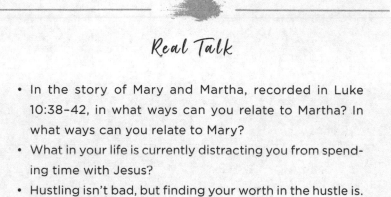

Real Talk

- In the story of Mary and Martha, recorded in Luke 10:38–42, in what ways can you relate to Martha? In what ways can you relate to Mary?
- What in your life is currently distracting you from spending time with Jesus?
- Hustling isn't bad, but finding your worth in the hustle is. What are practical ways in which you can remind yourself that when life gets crazy, being with Jesus is most important?

03

WHEN WE'RE AFRAID TO TRUST

My friend and I were laughing one day during a car ride as we listened to a song titled "Issues." We were seniors in college, and both of us had a history of horrible relationships with guys and friends. We doubted that God could speak to us. We had plenty of issues. We had trust issues. And we were tired of all the crap we had to deal with. Finally, I had found someone who was struggling like I was! But instead of working through the issues that hurt us and exhausted us . . . we laughed at them.

How hilarious. Right?

Wrong.

As silly as it sounds, I went to bed that night and stared at my wall. It was as if the wall were a screen on which I could watch my past playing out. I fast-forwarded to find all the moments that caused my trust issues. I watched my boyfriend cheat on me. I saw my friends talk bad about me and betray me. I relived the period in my life when I thought even God wasn't on my side.

My issues weren't so funny anymore. I cried into my sheets, realizing just how bad my trust issues were.

Why do we laugh at the pain that hurts us the most? Why do we hide our frustrations? Why do we just accept our trust issues instead of trying to work them out?

We tend to get overwhelmed by our trust issues and then exhaust ourselves with our doubts. We think we'll never be able to trust again. We feel alone because we've lied to ourselves and others for far too long.

My friend, I know how you feel. You will have days you dread. You will be overwhelmed and annoyed. You will feel frustrated. But understand this: *faith is not about having a perfect life; it's about having a trusting life.*

You can realize that not everyone will hurt you. Yes, some people have done things that hurt you. But God is doing something new.

You can trust that God is good at being God. He is sovereign, and He is in control. You don't need to fully understand how that works to trust Him.

You can trust that God wants to use what you have. Right now. As you are. With Him on your side, you can overcome any doubt, rough past, or difficult trial.

Trusting God to Fight Our Battles

There's a story in the Bible about a young man named David who faced a giant named Goliath. No one thought David would win. David was too small to wear the armor King Saul provided him, so he faced Goliath with only a slingshot and five stones. I can visualize David setting the armor aside when I read this part of the story:

David fastened on his sword over the tunic and tried walking around, because he was not used to them.

"I cannot go in these," he said to Saul, "because I am not used to them." So he took them off. Then he took his staff in his hand, chose five smooth stones from the stream, put them in the pouch of his shepherd's bag and, with his sling in his hand, approached the Philistine. (1 Samuel 17:39–40)

Even though young David was preparing to face a giant, he chose not to go into battle with something that did not feel right. That's a powerful picture for me. Often when I am overwhelmed and struggling, I have the opportunity to put on characteristics or things that don't feel right.

I put on passive-aggressiveness instead of truth.

I put on exhaustion instead of eagerness.

I put on fake compliments instead of genuine kindness.

I put up walls with God instead of trusting.

Was it riskier for David to confront Goliath without wearing the king's armor? Yes. But David wanted to use what he felt right about. He wanted to use what God gave him, not what someone else gave him.

David faced Goliath, trusting that God was on his side. He trusted that God was good. David did not know how God would intervene. He did not have the details or the play-by-play . . . but he still chose to trust God.

Goliath was much bigger and stronger than David, but Goliath didn't have God on his side. Because of that, David proved to be bigger and stronger than the giant. With one well-placed stone from his slingshot, David defeated Goliath. As he stood over the fallen giant, there was no doubt about who in that battle was bigger and stronger: God.

My friend, I know you are facing a hard week. Life has been kicking you in the butt. You have a painful past and a lot to do in the present, and you can't seem to catch a break. Your Goliath is big. Your week will be tiring. You will battle against that hard past, difficult trial, and challenging trust issue. But you can't just give up. You need to face your trust issues with whatever God has given you. Trust God to fight your battles for you and with you.

Do not try to be someone else and wear armor that only weighs you down. Embrace the strength of your Savior. Yes, the five small stones you carry might not seem like much for the battle you are facing, but remember: David won the battle with one small stone. Like David, you have a big God. And your big God is bigger than your biggest trust issue.

David did not know how God would intervene. But he knew God would. So he did not run away from the fight. He grabbed a weapon and confronted his opponent. He didn't know what God would do, but he stood there and trusted that God would do what was right.

One of the challenges of trusting God is that we aren't given a timeline. We aren't promised that Goliath will fall on the first stone—or at all. But trust is about standing there and deciding, *I'm ready to fight because I know I have Jesus.*

"If It Doesn't Challenge You, It Won't Change You!"

I was in bad shape physically post-graduation, so I started working out at a gym called Orangetheory. One of the trainers was named Nick, and I swear he could convince me to go to war. He yelled motivational quotes that pushed our group to work harder. One time he shouted an encouragement that stuck with me beyond the workout: "If it doesn't challenge you, it won't change you!"

I often forget that pain brings strength and battles bring triumph. Instead, I tend to laugh in the car at my Goliaths and avoid going to battle. I am often too tired to show up to fight, and that choice causes me to miss out on a true relationship with Jesus. Because without trust, what kind of relationship do you truly have?

We often look at our Goliaths and ask, "Why, God?" instead of declaring, "God's got this!" We think of challenges as overwhelming instead of as opportunities to see God. We see our pain as a pushback, not a challenge.

If God can lead David to triumph over Goliath, then surely He can get you through your hard week, your painful breakup, your horrible class, your impossible job, or your bad day. But it is up to *you* to show up to the fight.

Stop laughing off your trust issues and giving up on the fight. Show up to the battle, and stand there with confidence and trust. Bring your weapons to the battlefield, and know that God is already there. He will fight your battles for you and help you trust again.

Real Talk

- Read the entire story of David and Goliath in 1 Samuel 17. What made David different from Goliath? What made David different from the other people in the story?
- What trust issues are you currently facing?
- What is your typical response to trust issues? Do you tend to laugh at them, ignore them, deal with them, or something else?
- Have you ever become so exhausted from a challenge that you didn't show up to fight? If so, why did you give up?
- The next time you face a Goliath-like trust issue, what is your plan of attack?

04

WHEN WE WEAR LABELS

About a year ago I saw a Free People dress on sale at Dillard's. It was my lucky day! The next Sunday, I wore the dress to church. My new flowy white dress made me feel so trendy—like I was on the set of *Mamma Mia!*

Some girls have dresses that make them feel like a million bucks. That's what this dress did for me.

Until a sixth-grade girl saw me.

"Grace," she said, pausing to determine how best to complete her thought. "This dress doesn't look like your style."

What? This beautiful dress didn't look like it could be *my* style? What did she mean by that?

In the aftermath of her minor, not-that-important comment, I wrestled with wondering, *What is my style?* (Obviously, I needed a hobby.)

I get it—my style is not hippie; I wear too many basic Target dresses for that. I'm not a preppy girl. I sometimes wear flare jeans and satin shirts if I'm feeling spunky. Some people from college would say I dress "comfy," which is a nice way of saying I wear big T-shirts and Nike shorts. (The truth is that I dress like that only once a week. Okay, twice a week.)

So, what is my style? Some days I wear all black like I am emo. Others, I wear a pink blazer or funky pants. *How would others label me?*

I have an obsession with labels and how others stereotype me. My friends know I love to ask, "What did you first think of me when we met?" Part of it is my human desire to care about my worldly labels. And I struggle with labeling myself and others.

The Labels That Define Us

When I was in high school, I was very much known as the Christian girl. I went to a public high school, and I am thankful for the lessons I learned. If I am being really honest with you, sometimes I was the judgy Christian. Don't get me wrong—I started some great ministries and used the opportunity of being at a public school as a way to evangelize. But I did judge people more than I am proud of. I judged others who lived differently than me and those I didn't understand. This was not living the way Jesus taught us to live.

One time a peer I did not know well reached out to me. He lived in a different area than I did. Let's call him Kevin. Kevin and I hadn't spent much time together, but he called me out of the blue one morning.

"Hey, Grace." His voice was trembling. "I know you don't know me well. But are you busy right now?"

"Nope. Need something?"

"Yes, a ride to the doctor."

We didn't have a close enough relationship where I felt comfortable poking around for answers, so I just went to pick him up. He was around my age but lived in a different city from me. I knew he was gay, and—being completely honest—that was the label I had placed on him. All I really knew about Kevin was that he was gay. I am ashamed that I labeled his entire identity as his sexual orientation.

When Kevin got in my car, he told me he believed he had a sexually transmitted disease. He had called me because his parents would be crushed to learn that he was gay. He was in physical pain and needed help.

We tried and failed to get Kevin in with two doctors before deciding to go to the emergency room. We thought it would be difficult to convince the emergency room personnel to take an unsupervised fifteen-year-old who would require testing in a very personal area. Also, Kevin was embarrassed and ashamed because of the reason he was there.

However, the hospital staff were angels and made sure Kevin was taken care of and received the medicine he needed. While in the hospital, I listened to Kevin tell his story. I saw Kevin beyond the label I had falsely trusted to define what I needed to know about him. In that emergency room, I saw past that label and got to know a fifteen year-old boy who was bullied at his school, had a broken heart from a past relationship, and felt alone and too ashamed to talk to his family about his struggles.

Kevin told me that Christians were not always nice to him, but he wanted to know God more. We prayed together. When I opened my eyes after our prayer, I saw a brother in Christ. I saw a child of Christ's whom He yearned for. I no longer trusted that label to tell me Kevin's whole story.

The world teaches us to trust labels. We think stereotyping people is wise, when in fact wisdom is gained only through God Himself. The Enemy wants us to label others, and our human instinct tells us to trust these labels.

Trusting God requires releasing knowledge that the world gives us. Once you trust God, you realize this world is the closest to hell you will ever experience. It is full of sin. It is full of pain. And the labels the world gives us are temporary and untruthful.

When you meet someone, it's easy to hastily put together a file on them to store in your brain for easy access, like I did with Kevin. We allow our main—and often first—thought to become how we define that person. We choose to trust the label the world gives them.

"I know this girl once did this at a party. Therefore, she is a _____."

"I know this guy struggles with _____, so he is no good."

"I know this girl has a job that is _____, so that defines her."

But if we want see people the way God sees them, we must learn to look past the labels.

Jesus Looked Past the Labels

One of my favorite stories in the Bible is when Jesus decided to be a guest at the home of Zacchaeus, a tax collector.

> Jesus entered Jericho and was passing through. A man was there by the name of Zacchaeus; he was a chief tax collector and was wealthy. He wanted to see who Jesus was, but because he was short he could not see over the crowd. So he ran ahead and climbed a sycamore-fig tree to see him, since Jesus was coming that way.
>
> When Jesus reached the spot, he looked up and said to him, "Zacchaeus, come down immediately. I must stay at your house today." So he came down at once and welcomed him gladly.
>
> All the people saw this and began to mutter, "He has gone to be the guest of a sinner."

But Zacchaeus stood up and said to the Lord, "Look, Lord! Here and now I give half of my possessions to the poor, and if I have cheated anybody out of anything, I will pay back four times the amount."

Jesus said to him, "Today salvation has come to this house, because this man, too, is a son of Abraham. For the Son of Man came to seek and to save the lost." (Luke 19:1–10)

Tax collectors in this time period were known for being sleazy about money and stealing from others by overcharging them. They were living off a career that caused them to do not-so-great things. I once heard a preacher compare tax collectors to modern-day pimps.

But when Jesus encountered Zacchaeus, He did not label him as a sleazy tax collector. Instead, He trusted God to label Zacchaeus. Jesus basically said, "I know the world labels you this way, but I desire to sit and hang out with you."

Was Zacchaeus in an occupation that was sinful? Yes. But was he more than his occupation? Also yes. His occupation was not his identity. His occupation came from the world. His identity came from Jesus.

We struggle with trusting God's plan, trusting friends, and trusting in general. However, I truly believe we will never be able to trust anything or anyone until we stop trusting in worldly stereotypes.

Until you are able to give only God the power to name you and others, you will never be able to fully trust Him.

We All Carry Labels

I made a bad mistake in eighth grade. Our class was taking a standardized test, and I looked ahead. If you're anything like me, you tell people when you mess up. Rumors then changed the story to, "Grace purposely cheated on the biggest test and googled answers in the bathroom."

I began to be labeled as "Grace Valentine, cheater."

I was in eighth grade, and life went on. But that "cheater" label defined me for the rest of my time in middle school. As a result, I labeled myself a cheater too.

When I grew older and messed up with guys, I labeled myself as "dirty." Because of one mistake, I could not forgive myself for a long time. I thought one moment defined me more than Jesus' life did. I carried the weight of my bad reputation into college, where I was a party girl. Well, the "party girl" couldn't be seen at church. That would be like seeing a monkey in the desert.

We all carry labels. Sometimes we call these labels *reputations* and give our reputation the power to write not only our past but also our future. When we give anything from the world the power to name us and identify us, we basically are telling God, "I don't trust what You say about me. I trust what the world says more."

When people label you, let them. Let them talk about you. Let them judge you. Let them say their mean thoughts. But never, ever believe them. Don't waste your time justifying something Christ has already named. Christ has named you "loved," "forgiven," "friend," and "child." I believe when Jesus Christ cried out, "It is finished" on the cross (John 19:30), He meant it. Now, it is our turn to trust that the cross is more powerful than the world and our sins.

Trust Jesus to Name You What You Truly Are

Jesus invited Himself over to Zacchaeus's home, and He desires to invite you over to the place He is preparing for you. Jesus also desires to invite the girl or guy you judge. Actually, Jesus desires to stay at their house, the place where they sin, and the place where they sit alone and question their identity.

Jesus doesn't say, "If you meet Me at church, then we will talk, and I will begin to see your desire to change. Give Me five business days, and I will get back to you about your new name." Instead, Jesus says, "I want to meet you where you are. Let's hang out. I'm on My way. You have a name in My book. Now, let Me tell you what I have named you."

Jesus sees you. You might be surrounded by people who judge you. You might be surrounded by people who define you by your bad moment, your occupation, your past, or even your present actions. But Jesus is walking up to you, asking to meet you where you are.

Will you take your first step toward Him? Zacchaeus had heard about Jesus and decided to climb a tree to see Him. What if Zacchaeus were too ashamed by His past to look for Jesus? What if he had cared more about the gossip going on about him than he did about seeing Jesus?

Zacchaeus climbed the tree not only out of curiosity but also out of boldness. In that moment, meeting Jesus was more important than attempting to do anything about the gossip.

I struggle with this. When others judge me or gossip about me, I hide. I avoid them. I avoid the rumors, and in effect, I avoid living. But Jesus doesn't want you to hide in your room. He wants you to approach Him despite the hurtful words from your community. He wants you to climb your tree. Your tree may start with being honest with your peers about your struggles, calling a leader from church, or finally praying for the first time in a while. Make that move. Climb that tree to see Him. He will be waiting with an invitation in hand.

Promise me this: you will trust Jesus to give you your identity. Only He can name you as you truly are. He desires for you to leave your sin, but He meets you in your mess. Allow Him to place His label on you, and trust that what He believes about you is factual. The world is filled with lies, but His beliefs are true.

Perhaps my style of clothing does not fit one label. I might never become a fashion blogger. But I don't trust the world to put me in a box. Maybe someone like me can live boldly and meet Jesus daily, despite what others may say. I serve a Savior who has given me the most beautiful label of all time: a child of the King of kings.

Where's my crown? I'm wearing that with my favorite white dress.

Real Talk

- Do you feel like the world has given you a label? If so, what is that label? Who gave it to you?
- Read 1 Samuel 16:7. This was something the Lord said to Samuel. If you read this verse as if God were telling you this, what would it tell you about how God names you?
- Do you ever look back on your sin and forget to trust that God has forgiven you? If so, describe how that affects your relationship with God and others.
- Write a prayer asking God to remind you to trust Him to be the One who labels you. Thank Jesus for always meeting you where you are and for desiring for you to live with Him daily. Pray you can trust in His truth daily.

05

WHEN PEOPLE DON'T LIKE US

A couple of years ago, I was getting anxious because there was a woman at work who I felt did not like me. The worst, right? I mean, I knew I was going to see her almost every day. There was no avoiding this conflict. I would drive to work nervous about how our interaction would go that day. At first my thoughts were more positive . . . *Maybe today's the day she's going to realize I'm awesome and we can be friends! She'll see my new skirt and say, "Oh, girl, I love your skirt. Where's it from?" And I'll explain, "It's from my favorite online shop!" Then we'll giggle about sales, shopping, and become best friends.*

Yep, that never happened.

Then my thoughts became more negative. I began hoping we would just avoid any interaction. Sad, but true. One time I purposely avoided being on the elevator with just her. I legit pivoted and sat in the bathroom till I knew the elevator had left. Am I proud of this? No.

I consistently noticed signs that she did not like me. For example, she would be silent and ignore me if I spoke. I would ask for her advice, and she would walk away after a one-word reply or shrug. She also seemed to talk down to me. All this is my presumption, though—she never keyed my car or did anything drastic. I almost wish she had because I think I exhausted myself more wondering if she liked me.

When I told someone about my concerns, my friend laughed and said, "Yeah, I see that."

Other people had assumed that she did not like me as well!

Am I unlikable?

How can I convince her to change her mind about me?

Maybe if I say this, she will respect me.

Maybe if I compliment her, she will think I want to be her friend.

Maybe if I help her with this, she will finally like me.

Maybe if I avoid her, she will just magically forget that my presence annoys her.

Nothing gave me the response I desired. We did not end up becoming best friends.

One day I woke up and realized I was wasting my time.

I did not have to convince her that I am worthy. I did not have to persuade her to like me. I didn't even have to waste my time trying to avoid her in an elevator. In fact, I was wasting time trying to be someone she would like when I could have focused on being like Jesus—living a life focused on love and kindness, not on people-pleasing, convincing, and persuading.

The Cross Matters More

If I hold someone's opinion about me so high that her not liking me causes me anguish, then I am saying the cross is not enough. But the truth is, the cross matters more. Jesus stretching out His arms and dying for us matters more.

Jesus saying, "Come as you are" matters more than people not liking us. If we decide to value others' opinions more than we value the cross, we are saying that we do not trust God with what He created in us.

We need to learn how to deal with people not liking us. Yes, it hurts. And yes, it causes distrust. But God wants more from us. It's time for us to stop exhausting ourselves because of others' opinions and start living in the truth from God.

I wish I could tell you everyone liked me, but that would be a lie. A big one!

Sadly, some people don't like me. Sometimes people don't like me for no reason. Sometimes it is for a reason. And sometimes it is for a reason I can't help. Don't get me wrong—I have plenty of flaws and haven't always been the kindest gal. But I'm not awful. Yet some people out there just don't like me. I wish I could flip my hair and laugh it off. I wish I could mean it when I say, "I don't care." But the truth is, I struggle because I care what people think of me. I can't be the only one, can I?

How to Handle People Who Don't Like Us

Maybe you are like me, and there are some people who don't like you. Maybe you, too, have someone at work who doesn't like you, and no matter what you do, Emily always has to tell Janet her two cents about you.

You can't win. So if, like me, you are sometimes infected with people-pleasing, read on. If you also find yourself upset when people don't like you, this is for you. Here are my three tips on how to handle those who are just not that into us.

1. Let them talk.

If people don't like you, then let them talk. I get why this is difficult. If you're like me, you love a good clapback and speaking your mind. But speaking your mind is not always biblical. Speaking your mind gives the Enemy an opportunity to take someone else's sin and cause you to lose self-control and say something hurtful. When you do this, you are giving someone's sin the power to cause you to sin.

If we allow someone's negative words to become our identity, we are sinning. When we believe their words, we are rejecting the truth Jesus already proclaimed over us when He died on the cross for us.

When someone talks about us, let's let them. Don't fight it. The world may tell us that we need a good clapback, but Jesus says let them talk.

Their words are lies. They are distractions that deserve love, not a frustrated clapback. We do not need to justify ourselves to someone else's sin.

2. Prioritize love and grace above trust.

We are called to love and give grace to everyone but not necessarily to trust everyone. Trust comes from wisdom and discernment, while grace and love come from the cross. The cross has been finished, so, yes, we are called to love and give grace. But trust comes from wisdom given through prayer and life experiences God has granted us. We do not have to trust the people who hurt us. But we do have to forgive them.

3. Learn to trust again.

Now, I know this appears to contradict what I just said, but hear me out. The more you and I look back on our past hurts, the more we miss out on present love. It is not fair or fun for us to assume that everyone is talking about us. Time doesn't heal all wounds. But Jesus does.

If you were hurt years ago, you can learn to trust again. You don't have to trust the same people who hurt you, but trust the people God puts in your life now. Stop exhausting yourself with the assumption that you will never find people worthy of trust. Stop exhausting yourself with the lie that you are a bother. You are God's creation, and you are here for a reason. If your desire is to have godly friendships that reflect Him, He will give them to you—in His timing.

Look to Jesus for Your Worth

This might be a struggle you're dealing with right now. Maybe someone at work doesn't like you. Maybe it's someone in your friend group. Maybe it's even a family member. I get it. You're hurt. You're frustrated. You're upset. It's not a sin to experience any of those emotions. But, please, never allow your identity to depend on someone else's mean thoughts about you.

When you allow someone's sin to write your identity, you are rejecting God's truth. You were created for a purpose. You are worthy of friendships that are true and reflect Jesus. You are not your past, your reputation, the lies people say about you, or even the thoughts they think about you. Look to Jesus for your worth.

If you can't find anyone who will be kind to you, then choose to be someone who is kind. Learn to give grace. Be the one who loves like Jesus in a dark world.

Sin is contagious, but so is joy.

Real Talk

- Have you experienced anxiety over someone not liking you? Or have you spent too much time wondering, *Does this person like me?* If so, how did you feel? To what extent did your anxiety consume your thoughts?
- Why do you think you allow other people's opinions to hold so much value?
- What is one way you can trust God's view of you over the opinions of others?
- What point in this chapter resonated with you the most? What is one practical takeaway you can use from that point?

Part 2

AM I THE ONLY ONE WHO FEELS HURT AND LONELY?

06

WHEN WE'VE
BEEN HURT

I have been rejected. I have been betrayed. I have been let down, and I have been hurt. It's universal—that feeling you get in the pit of your stomach when someone doesn't like you. The thoughts that race when you know someone is talking about you. The feeling of disappointment when someone you thought you could trust and love does something that feels like a slap in the face.

That's the worst feeling. But it's an inevitable feeling. People hurt you. People wrong you. And it is exhausting to open your heart to others when you have been hurt.

I have been the subject of gossip and rumors that were clearly untrue. I have been hurt by family members. I have been hurt by friends, exes, and even lies I've told myself. Some have been trivial; others have anguished me.

Hurt sucks.

I often get hurt by rejection, and sometimes this can be trivial. Some of my best friends know how hurt I was by one guy. All he did to hurt me was not text me back. Yes, I did say this was trivial.

I went on a couple of dates with a boy who told me he would like to see me again. Then he decided to never text me or reach out to me again.

But he said he wanted to see me again!

Maybe he texted me while I was on a plane and I didn't receive it, and now he won't text because he thinks I rejected him.

I didn't see him again until we bumped into each other at the grocery store. The worst part is, I thought I recognized him but brushed it off. *No chance*, I thought and casually continued on my way to get my sea salt chips. Turns out, it was him. He actually was excited to see me and kind to me. I was more awkward than a freshman-year homecoming picture.

I fumbled over my words. The conversation went something like this:

Me: "How are you doing?"

Him: "I'm doing great! Work has been busy, but other than that, enjoying this great weather! How have you been? How's the book?"

Me: "It is good! I'm doing good. . . . How are you?"

I've already asked that question.

I scrambled to add something else to make up for my mistake.

"Well, my family is in town, so I've gotta go. Good seeing you!"

My family was not in town, and he probably knew that. I laughed with my friends about my embarrassing encounter and said, "This is what happens once you hurt me—I can't look at you without fumbling over my words."

Then one friend reminded me, "His rejection did not hurt you; you didn't even like him that much. The rejection hurt you because it reminded you of other hurts you had bottled up."

Well, that conversation sure took a quick turn! But my friend was correct. I tend to freak out over something trivial because it makes me reflect on deeper issues I have never dealt with in a healthy way.

Ten Truths About Our Past Hurts

Reflection helps us look back on our past and see God's hand in the mess. If you do not reflect on your hurts, you will get hurt more, and over trivial things. Your wound will sting if it has not been dressed and treated. If you are like me and avoid reflection, it's time to put your big-girl panties on. We are about to reflect on our past hurts and work through ten truths we need to keep in mind.

1. Our past hurts are in the past.

If I held up a full water bottle for ten seconds, my arm would be fine. If I held up that same water bottle for an hour, I could probably do it, but my arm would slack. If I tried to hold that same water bottle for twelve hours, my arm would feel like it's about to fall off! Not because the water bottle would be heavy, but because it would be burdensome.

We all have past hurts. We have all dealt with betrayal. We have watched people come and go. However, if we hold on to pain, betrayal, and grudges, we'll only exhaust ourselves. We can't have arms that are open for others when we are busy holding our burdens.

Run to Jesus. Trust in Jesus. What has happened is in the past. Don't look back. Focus on what Jesus is doing in your life now. Focus on bringing your burdens to Him. Jesus said, "Come to me, all you who are weary and burdened, and I will give you rest" (Matthew 11:28).

2. Time doesn't heal all wounds, but Jesus does.

Time will not heal our pain, but there's a remedy that is better and more effective—Jesus. Spending time with Him allows us to see the bigger picture.

Let me be real with you: your frustrations may be valid. Your hurt is real. Your pain is big. But sitting around and complaining will not bring you peace. Waiting for time to heal your wounds will not heal your pain. Run to Jesus for comfort. I promise, if you don't sit at His feet, you will still be hurt years later.

For me, a dumb relationship in high school caused me trust issues for years. I thought I wouldn't care years later. Truth was, I did care. I was still hurt. I was hurt because I bottled up my pain and thought time alone would help. But then I would experience another rejection that would make me reflect back on my past hurt.

If you and I desire to be able to move on, we must bring our past hurts to the ultimate Healer. If Jesus can heal the blind, then He can help us find peace again after being hurt. "He heals the brokenhearted and binds up their wounds" (Psalm 147:3 ESV).

3. Worrying and frowning give us wrinkles.

I ain't got the money to get Botox! So on a much lighter note, smile. Smile because worry lines will not be the cutest. Laugh lines we can deal with because they're worth the joy. Worrying only wastes our time and energy, and it gives us wrinkles.

4. We aren't what someone did to us. We are what Jesus did for us.

Jesus loves you, and He loves me. A perfect Savior considers us worth saving. This is not because of anything we did but because of who He is. Instead of finding our worth in the people who hurt us, let's find peace in knowing that Jesus loved us enough. His love can overcome death, so I think His love can overcome our hurts.

I remember hearing negative opinions about me before I moved to a new city.

"Grace is not qualified for the position she was offered . . . she's too young and not ready for this. She's also loud and a bit too much."

I had been an intern the year before at this job and received a full-time offer, which I accepted. My start date was three days after my college graduation. I was planning to move the day after I graduated. When people in the town found out that I was coming back and my summer internship was extended to a full-time offer, I received a lot of support. I received a lot of love. However, I also remember hearing from a friend that some people thought I was not qualified for the job. She told me this so I would know that I had "people to prove wrong" and that "Grace, you will show them!" She told me their thoughts to push me to be my best, but hearing that others were talking about me in a negative way just made me anxious. I was anxious about the opinions of others and hurt by their actions. I exhausted myself over-thinking the effects of their gossip. But then one day I felt Jesus tell me, *I call you "Love."* Jesus loves me, and He calls me by His love. That is my name. His precious love overflows. The hurt may still be there, but it is not as painful because I have Him.

When a boyfriend cheated on me, I had to remind myself I was not a second option to Jesus. He never turned His back on me. I found peace in knowing that what Jesus did for me is truth and how that guy treated me was simply a distraction from my true worth.

5. There will be happy days again.

I am a firm believer that every valley leads to a mountain and every thunderstorm leads to a rainbow. You might be having a bad day, but bad days help us appreciate happy days. Some of your best days haven't happened yet. You will get through the hurt. But there is always something to look forward to. God is working for your good, which is His good. God is working behind the scenes. Through every hurt, every tiring day, every pain, and every rejection, His good is being revealed. "We know that in all things God works for the good of those who love him, who have been called according to his purpose" (Romans 8:28).

6. There is probably a song to help us cope with the pain.

When I go through hurt, pain, and betrayal, I listen to music that helps release my feelings. I once met a girl who asked me what music I listen to when I want to feel God again after pain. I answered,

"Country music." She laughed and said something along the lines of, "I thought you were going to say a worship song."

After a breakup, do I run first to "Oceans" by Hillsong? No. After I lost a job, do I run to Bethel Music? No, I do not. I run to country singers who, whether they are believers or not, have God-given gifts for creating music that touches the heart. I lie on my bed, listen to a good song, and watch my fan spin above me. There is nothing wrong with appreciating the gifts God has given others.

Don't get me wrong: when you are hurt, I pray you run to Scripture, prayer, and Jesus' feet. But scream to Tim McGraw, Taylor Swift, Darius Rucker, Thomas Rhett, or even Lizzo or whatever type of music helps you. Processing your hurt is easier when there is music already written that relates to your thoughts. What a gift we have in music.

7. We may never know why.

I often say, "I just need closure." The truth is, I'm not looking for closure but simply an answer as to why something happened to me.

We have to learn to accept that we may never receive the answers we so desperately want. We may never know why he left, why our friend betrayed us, or why the employer chose someone else. We should find peace not in answers but in the One who is in control.

You may never know the answer to "Why?" But that is okay. I would much rather know the answer to "Who?" God is the One who is in control. That gives me closure. We can move on when we trust that God is at work through our pain.

8. God is doing something new.

Today might be exhausting, but we will be stronger because of it. Yesterday could have been a hurtful day, but today is new, and we are closer to our blessing. God is always at work. We need to trust that God is doing something new in our lives—and if our vision is blurry, it is probably because we lost focus on the real target.

9. A tear today is a "thank-You" to God tomorrow. ——

Your tears are leading you to your blessings. You may not know why now, but you will see God's goodness. One of my favorite scriptures is "Rejoice always, pray continually, give thanks in all circumstances; for this is God's will for you in Christ Jesus" (1 Thessalonians 5:16–18).

When you are hurt, rejoice anyway. When you feel the anguish and pain of betrayal, pray through it. And with every tear, celebrate. Even when your life isn't going the way you want, celebrate that God's will is being accomplished.

One day you and I will both see this through and realize that God's will is always right. The tears we experience today are simply a path to our "thank-You" to God later.

Trust His faithfulness more than you wrestle with bitterness. Find eagerness and peace in who He is. God is faithful, and His will is best.

10. Everyone has been hurt, but not everyone has —— been healed.

Look around. There are people around you who need your testimony.

One day you will meet someone suffering the same pain you experienced. On that day, I don't think you will wish that God had spared you from the hurt. I don't think you will wish that someone else had to go through what you went through. I don't think you will wish that you had slept through the pain.

I think in that moment you will find out why we as Christians are called to more than believing. We are called to share what Jesus has done on the cross and what He has done for us. And when you have the opportunity to tell others about the heartache, pain, and hurt you have felt, you will see that God was simply preparing you for His work. Your pain will turn into someone else's answered prayer because they will finally know someone who not only understands but can point them to true healing.

No one says hurt is fun. But your hurt today is your testimony tomorrow. Allow God to intercede on your bad days. Trust that finding your energy in Him gets you through the tough times. Eat ice cream, laugh about your pain, and dance to breakup songs. But also pray. God is at work in your life.

Real Talk

- Read 1 Thessalonians 5:16–18. Think about a hurt you currently have. How can you take that hurt and (1) rejoice, (2) pray, and (3) give thanks and trust? Write out tangible ways for each point.
- When have you used your past hurts to help someone? How did it make you feel to be able to help someone from your experience?
- When has someone used their past hurts to help you? What role did their experience play in helping you?
- Is it difficult for you to trust God when dealing with hurt? Why or why not?
- Which of the ten truths in this chapter resonated with you the most? Why?

07

WHEN WE ACCEPT BEING TREATED BADLY

"Seriously—what am I doing wrong?"

I was on FaceTime with Sam, my best guy friend from college. Sam had the pleasure of dealing with all my boy issues.

I was venting to Sam about one guy in particular who had taken me on multiple dates. I had even met his family, and he had sent me the winky face emoji *multiple* times. (Modern-day flirting, I presume?)

But there was one thing he had not done. One thing that I would've liked after at least the second date.

He had not kissed me.

I know what some of you are thinking: *That's so sweet of him, Grace. Why would this bother you? Aren't you a good Christian girl with healthy boundaries? How kind and patient of him!*

Well, this boy ain't no Jesus Christ, so don't misunderstand this story. After he first reached out to me, I tried the typical girl tactic where I asked mutual friends all about him. The results were not great.

"I don't really see you two together . . . but, I mean, he's nice!"

I got mixed feedback about him. Some people raved about him, and some people warned me to be careful. Nothing scares a girl "investigating" more than the words "be careful." He was different from me, and some said he was more of a partyer than me. Hey, he was over twenty-one, so to each their own, but maybe not my style. He also had an ex-girlfriend who was the complete opposite of me. She was more of a partyer and was described as "chill." Something I will never be—chill. Oh, and his ex-girlfriend was very pretty. How annoying, right? How dare she be pretty! (Note my sarcasm.)

Let me just say to every girl who is like me and likes to investigate someone's whole life before a first date . . . stop. I realized two things shortly into my investigation:

1. It is not fair to the guy that I can send four texts and learn every mistake he's ever made. Thank goodness he only saw post-college Grace. Stop judging people by their pasts. You can use wisdom and their past as a way to protect yourself, but don't allow it to be something you trust.
2. This investigation only caused me to be awkward, not myself, and fooled by my expectations.

I remember thinking that I would need to establish boundaries with him. I remember being nervous that he was going to expect something from me that I would not give. I was already assuming that this guy would treat me in a way that valued my body more than me.

But there I was, a couple of dates later, unkissed and confused.

Does he not like me?

Am I not attractive enough?

Why does he keep seeing me when I'm giving him nothing? What's in this for him?

One time he texted me when he was in town and asked if I wanted to hang out. I told him he could come over to my house after I ate dinner with a friend. Let me be clear: I was not booty-calling him. I also wanted a low-pressure hangout. I would be lying, though, if I said I didn't anticipate that this low-pressure hangout would end in a kiss.

But this guy had other plans.

"I'm trying to think of places you haven't been to in town!" he said, then suggested we get breakfast at a restaurant he wanted to try.

I invited the guy to my house at night, and he insisted on picking me up and taking me to a restaurant for breakfast instead. What had the world come to?

Don't get me wrong: he was a great, respectful guy. He was a little sneaky, but I just don't think we were meant to be. However, he was never misleading toward me. He was never unkind. He never used me. He always respected me.

Every time I tried to figure out what the disappointment of a no-kiss meeting meant, it only led me to one conclusion: he respected me.

Why was that so foreign to me?

I think most twentysomething women would be surprised if a guy did *not* kiss them. And maybe the problem isn't the guy. Maybe it's the dating culture we have become accustomed to. We have settled for people who use us. Here I was, getting tired because of a boy who didn't kiss me when I should have been tired of how surprised I was that he hadn't kissed me. I wondered when I had become so negative about what guys wanted from me.

For some reason, respect from a guy had become foreign to me. I was confused by a guy who wanted to get to know my personality before my body. I was confused by a guy buying my dinner and not touching my leg. I was confused by an "experienced" guy not pushing me to experience anything with him, except for a good breakfast. (We experienced that a couple of times!)

The Lies We Tell Ourselves

This chapter really isn't about a guy not kissing me. This chapter is about everyone, no matter your relationship, no matter your life situation, no matter your occupation, who—like me—has simply accepted being treated like crap because we view ourselves in a crappy way.

That does not sound profound. But think about it this way—we have all accepted being treated badly because deep down we have thought:

That's just the way our culture is. I'll never find anyone who treats me different.

I have to give something in order to receive kindness.

I have nothing worthwhile to offer.

Let's break down each of these lies.

1. "That's just the way our culture is. I'll never find ——— anyone who treats me different."

We have associated *different* with the word *extinct*. Different isn't bad, and different isn't rare. You can find a job that respects you as a woman in leadership. You can find a friend who doesn't betray you. You can find a guy who respects you and doesn't push boundaries. However, if you want different, you must do these three things:

- *Be different yourself.* If you live different, life will become different. Stop accepting less than different.
- *Stop thinking different is extinct.* Different isn't extinct; it is endangered. When an animal makes the endangered species list, humans protect it. When we find the species, we monitor and support it. Similarly, it's rare to be someone who lives a Christian life that changes the way you work, deal with finances, care about your health, and date. It is endangered in our society. When you see others doing the same, support them. The more

we encourage our fellow "differents," the more our endangered species can grow.

- *Stop thinking different is weird.* It wasn't weird that the guy didn't kiss me. I'm the one who made it seem weird. I say I want different, but then when different comes, I am suspicious. Trust that you deserve different. Trust that you are worth different. Trust that different will be given to you out of respect.

2. "I have to give something in order to receive kindness."

We live in a culture where love is earned, and if you want to be somebody, you have to possess something that makes you worthy. But Jesus died on the cross for us as the Author of love. Jesus died for us not because we deserved it, but because He loved us. On that day, true love was demonstrated in its highest form. True love isn't dependent on what we offer; it is dependent on our Savior.

I'm not saying that this boy who didn't kiss me was in love with me. But was this boy treating me in a loving way? Yes. I want to be loving to those I know well and call close friends. I want to be loving to strangers, new friends, and even acquaintances. I never want people to feel that the way I treat them depends on what they offer me.

3. "I have nothing worthwhile to offer."

I struggle with believing that looks are what I offer guys. I struggle with believing the lie that my value as a woman is dependent on my body. Don't get me wrong. I know the right answers. My first book was about how we are "enough" because of Jesus. This world tells us often that looks matter, but our worth is much greater than being a pretty face.

I still struggle to believe this. Before a first date, I worry about whether I look "fat." At college formals, I was the girl who felt ugly next to my skinny, size-0 friends in their tight dresses. But deep down, I know my worth comes from an everyday relationship with Jesus.

Confidence isn't a destination. You don't arrive at confidence and live in a happily-ever-after land where you never jump into your skinny jeans and wonder if you've gained a few. There is no magic pill that will make you 100 percent content for the rest of your life. You have to choose confidence daily and live it out daily. It is up to you to decide that you want to live with joy with what God gave you. We live in a broken world. If we want to defeat insecurity, we must come to Jesus daily.

This is for all the women who accept crap: Stop it. Stop accepting guys who use you. Stop accepting a job where people walk on you. Stop accepting friends who make you feel insecure instead of making you laugh. Look for different. And when you find it, don't be suspicious. I hate that it's so rare for someone to treat us in a loving way. Trust that it might be rare for someone to respect you, but respect is not extinct.

And when a guy doesn't kiss you, I hope you act differently than I did. Instead of FaceTiming your friends in a state of confusion, smile because respect isn't extinct. Smile because someone is treating you in a loving way. Smile because you are worth more, and anyone or anything that treats you differently is wrong.

Real Talk

- Have you been surprised by someone being respectful or kind to you when you didn't give them anything in return?
- Do you struggle to believe different is not extinct? Why?
- How have your past hurts affected the way you view yourself currently?
- What in your past makes it difficult for you to trust that you are worth more?

08

WHEN CHURCH PEOPLE HURT US

You see it in the news, or you hear it in your gossip group text: The pastor cheated on his wife. The church girls hurt someone's feelings. The "Christian" guy did something so horrible to your friend that she refuses to set foot in a church again.

It has happened to me, and it has happened to many.

Church people have hurt us.

I was in college when I overheard two Christian girls in the gym talking about one of my best friends in a negative and, honestly, disgusting way. These were "sweet" girls and apparently "good Christians." But their words were far from sweet. I couldn't help but wonder if all "good Christians" were like them.

Many years ago at a church, a pastor asked me (and only me) in front of a bunch of people if I had any "walk of shame" stories. I was the new girl and felt judged. He later told everyone he meant stories that I had witnessed in college, since I obviously seemed like I hung out with a different crowd than any of the others. Basically, I think he meant that I looked like a girl who would hang out with partyers. It was a weird statement, and I was definitely offended by whatever it meant.

When the pastor put me on the spot, I was embarrassed and ashamed. I answered that I once saw a girl climb through a window to sneak into her dorm early in the morning after a long night out. The truth was that I was that girl climbing through the window at 6:00 a.m. after a wild night. I said that to see how everyone would react. They laughed about this "girl" I knew. I don't think anyone's intentions were to make me feel judged. They were genuinely nice and kind people. However, in that moment, I felt targeted, judged, and dirty as the group laughed about "someone" sneaking in through a window. I remember thinking, *I will never be able to be honest with anyone at this church about my past.*

Jesus Is Perfect, but His Followers Aren't

I have learned from my non-Christian friends that they don't mind Jesus. In fact, they tend to agree with a lot of His teachings. They think Jesus was a good man.

One day I was talking to a friend who had great knowledge of Scripture but did not believe in Jesus. I asked what was stopping him from trusting in Jesus as his Savior. He looked at me and said, "Have you met most Christians and church people? They suck."

I tried to defend my people. "You just met some bad ones," I said. "They don't all suck."

Looking back, I realize my response might not have been correct.

Church people do suck. Church people sin. Pastors mess up and hurt those who look up to them. Christians gossip and judge. And churches have become an establishment for socializing more than a hospital for the broken.

After I responded to my friend with my quick answer, I realized that perhaps he was onto something. Why would my friend want to believe in a Savior when he's been hurt by people who worship that Savior? Why would anyone believe Jesus is powerful if He can't make those mean, judgmental college girls nice? Why would anyone want to be led by a pastor if he is going to hide a sin that hurts many people for years?

This is the tension we as believers face and those who are curious about Christianity encounter. Jesus is a perfect Savior, but His followers can hurt others. His followers *do* hurt others.

How should we respond?

How to Respond When Church People Hurt You

I want to address two groups of people. First, those who have been hurt by Christians and, as a result, struggle to trust Jesus and the church. Second, those on the receiving end of this question: How do we, as a church, respond to those who have been hurt?

To the one who has been hurt by Christians or a church . . . I am sorry.

I wish I could say this to you face-to-face. I have been the crappy Christian. I have been the hurtful Christian. But I have also learned that hurt people hurt others. The reason I lived a hurtful life was because of my pain and frustration, not because of my Savior. See, my Savior is the One who saved me from the life I have lived, not the One who condones how I have treated others.

I know you have been hurt, but I am asking you to do three things again.

1. Trust again.

Trust people again. I cannot promise you that you will not be hurt, but I can promise that God will continue to bring you closer to Him.

Walk back into church one more time. Perhaps a different church, or maybe the church you know you need to go back to. Wherever you go, do not give your old wounds the power to control you.

On Christmas Day when I was in the third grade, I fell off my bike and needed stitches. Santa had brought me a bike, and I went for a ride and busted my chin open. I was scared to ride a bike again until eighth grade. I had been hurt before. Why would I need to ride a bike, anyway? I was fine without it.

I felt God push me to go mountain biking at summer camp when I was sixteen years old. I fell again, actually. I still have a scar from that fall. But I kept trying.

When I was nineteen, I taught campers how to mountain bike. I still got nervous when they (or I) fell off the bike. But I also had fun. I created memories. I grew in strength and experienced adventure.

If you want a life of strength and adventure, you are going to have to get back on your bike. You are going to have to identify your past hurts and the potential to be hurt again. But realize that the risk is worth the adventure.

Trusting in humans and trying to find a Christian community will not always be easy. You might get hurt again. But you might learn something fun and wise. You might live a life that turns out to teach others how to do the same thing. When you trust again, you experience another opportunity to grow.

2. Try again.

After I watched Christians break their vows or promises to God and others, I couldn't help but think, *Why do I have to live a pure life?*

Following Jesus is not just for eternal life; it is for freedom today. Following Jesus doesn't just require obedience; it leads to obedience.

Try again not only to follow Jesus but to live in a way that respects the relationship you have with Him. You don't live this life because one of your leaders does; you live this life because it gives you the most freeing life today.

3. Pray about it again.

Instead of complaining about your hurt, run to your Savior. Even if you don't believe in Him, what do you have to lose by talking to Him? Nothing!

Talk to Him. Make bold requests of Him. Be honest about your hurts and the healing that you need. Ask Him to give you wisdom and to help you learn to trust Him and others. I promise, you will never regret praying. Pray even just one more time and give God an opportunity to respond to your hurts.

Yes, you've been hurt by others. But you've been loved by a Savior you might not even know yet. Don't give up just because you're frustrated and hurt. Trust that your Savior's love is real and life-changing and that you can find others who consistently strive to live a loving life. Do they still mess up? Of course they do. But they get stronger each day by learning and growing in their faith. These people will not be perfect, but they will be life-giving more than hurtful.

Next, *to the one who is a Christian and wonders how to respond to this question* . . . we must stop pretending.

We need to admit that Christians have flaws. There are flaws in our pastors and our leaders. There are flaws in our worship teams and in our congregations. We are not perfect, and we have not only sinned against God, but we have also sinned against God's children.

We have to ask for forgiveness and then listen to their hurt instead of responding with our opinions. It's tempting to respond to someone's hurt and say, "Not all Christians do that." Or, "But have you met *this* pastor?"

Don't get me wrong—you should present them with hope that Christians can love. But this love needs to be *shown* and not *told*. If someone has been hurt by Christians or by the church, she might be blind to seeing this love unless it is consistently shown to her. That is where you come in. Be the different one. Be the one who loves her well. You cannot be perfect, but you can consistently point her to our perfect Savior.

Ask this person for her story before you try to convince her that Christians are loving. Do not respond like I did, saying, "You just met bad ones." Listen to her. Jesus sat and ate with nonbelievers. He knew their stories. We can find out people's stories by listening, asking questions, and getting to know them.

Pursue Jesus, Not Perfection

Pursuing perfection is exhausting. As I look back on times when I witnessed or heard about pastors straying from their walk, especially now that I've worked full-time at a church, I see how easily sin can creep into anyone's life—especially those in a position of influence. We tend to hide our true feelings. We pursue perfection instead of Jesus. We "fake it until we make it," until our actions finally reveal we are not making it. Pursue Jesus, not perfection.

You cannot fake a pursuit of Jesus. You can lie for a while, but just like my cheap CVS makeup, your lies will not hide your flaws forever. Pursuing Jesus means that you boast in your weakness because your weakness proves that your Savior is strong (2 Corinthians 12:9). You pursue a life that reflects His love, not a life that pretends.

Christians and non-Christians, although we all fail, Jesus prevails. I promise a step toward Jesus is a step toward healing. You have been hurt, but you are loved today and every day. He will not fail you. Be the Christian who follows Him. Be the one who pursues Jesus instead of perfection.

Real Talk

- Have you been hurt by a church or a Christian? If so, did this hurt more than being hurt by a nonbeliever? Why or why not?
- Complete this statement: "I cannot be honest with people in the church because I am scared that _____."
- What effect would it have on unbelievers if we as a church started pursuing Jesus instead of perfection?
- What is one way you can trust in the church either more or again?

09

WHEN WE ARE
LEFT OUT

When I was a teenager, I dealt with friends breaking my trust repeatedly. Here are two memories I have of those experiences.

- *The group text that didn't include me.* I remember that sinking feeling in the pit of my stomach when I realized there was a group text my "best friends" were chatting in without me. The worst part was how I discovered I had been left out: they were in my car as I was driving, and I saw them talking bad about me. Yep, that made my stomach really hurt.
- *My "best friend" reading my text conversations with the guy I was dating.* My friend took my phone and read my texts. Then she took a screenshot of the texts, sent them to her phone, deleted the thread, and posted the screenshots in that group text

I had been left out of for all to read. Then they made fun of me. Yep, that scar still stings.

I think we all have trust issues with friends because of past hurts. I am a girl in her mid-twenties carrying scars from mean girls in high school. My friends in college often observed the side effects of those experiences.

I had forgotten how bad that pain in the gut felt until I went through the same experience again in college. My best friend, Britta, had set her phone on our bunk bed. (Yes, we had bunk beds in college—half off rent!) Her phone lit up, drawing my eyes to her screen. There it was again—all my best friends in a group text without me. I panicked. After crying, overreacting, and wondering what I did to deserve this cruel ordeal again, I asked Britta, "What did I do wrong? Just let me know. I saw the text without me."

Britta first looked confused. Then she laughed. I still was crying because I'm not chill.

"Grace, we were going to throw you a surprise birthday party," she answered. "Yours is in the summer, and you never get to celebrate it with us. And we wanted to do it around Mardi Gras because we know you miss being home in New Orleans during that time."

There I was, assuming my friends were talking crap about me when, in reality, they were loving me well. My trust issues were spilling onto people who had done nothing but love me.

We've All Been Hurt

We all have a past that affects how we see things in our present. We've all been hurt. We have scars, whether small or large, that are painful when anything makes contact with them and reminds us the wounds are still there.

It is okay to have been hurt. You do not have to be ashamed of the rejection you have experienced. However, I encourage you to acknowledge that God is doing something new in your life. I know you have been hurt, but you have also been loved. You have been loved by others and even admired by strangers walking past you. Stop giving the people who have hurt you the power to live in your present. God is doing something new!

Turn the Other Cheek

Jesus gave us advice on what to do when someone hurts us: "You have heard that it was said, 'Eye for eye, and tooth for tooth.' But I tell you, do not resist an evil person. If anyone slaps you on the right cheek, turn to them the other cheek also. And if anyone wants to sue you and take your shirt, hand over your coat as well" (Matthew 5:38–40).

This world will tell you that once you have been hurt, you should put up a wall. We believe the lie that protecting ourselves is being realistic and having trust issues is a normal part of life. But Jesus told us that when someone strikes our cheek, we should show them the other one. Jesus was saying that our love should always be louder than our trust issues.

Living a life of love means that you give grace when most people give a piece of their mind. Living a life of love means that you give gentle words when most people go off. Living a life of love means that you show self-control and wisdom through your words, actions, and even your thoughts. Living a life of love is not easy, but it does come more naturally when you are pursuing Jesus daily. Turning the other cheek means that you choose love and grace over revenge or pushing back. It is not easy, but it is purposeful.

Let me be clear: if someone is physically or emotionally abusive, walk away and get help. God wants you to seek healing, and if you have been abused, you need to step away from your abuser to seek healing. Abuse is when anyone is physically hurting you, consistently tearing you down with words that hurt you, or emotionally manipulating you. But if someone hurts you in a nonabusive way, which can be friend drama, a not-so-nice coworker, a family member tearing you down a couple times . . . reflect on it, know that it has happened, and love anyway. By nonabusive, I do not mean that these types of hurts do not stink. They still hurt. This feeling comes from betrayal, gossip, abandonment, and more. It hurts you, and the pain still stings. But grace is stronger than any pain we experience. Give grace when it is difficult. Give second chances even when you don't want to. And learn to love again.

"Don't Bleed on the Ones Who Didn't Cut You"

As the saying goes, "Don't bleed on the ones who didn't cut you." Turn your cheek after you get hurt, and expose yourself to love again. You will never experience good friendships if you don't release your trust issues.

When I reflect on the hurts I felt in middle school and high school, I realize that I am better because of the pain I experienced. For example, I am kinder now because I know what it's like to be the outcast.

When you reflect on your past hurts, choose to think of the strength they have brought you instead of dwelling on the issues they have caused. When you give your hurts to God, He gives you something more powerful than your past hurts—He gives you His Spirit. And His Spirit will give you strength to trust again.

Not everyone is out to get you. Not everyone will hurt you. I often think we call our trust issues "realistic," but we serve a God who is not that kind of realistic. It is not realistic, as we would define it, to turn your other cheek to someone who hurts you. But the gospel is crazy good that way. Walking in God's truth makes you do things that might not always be "realistic," but they are purposeful.

Real Talk

- What past hurts are you carrying?
- Is it difficult for you to "turn the other cheek" and trust again after being hurt? Why or why not?
- "Don't bleed on the ones who didn't cut you." What does this saying mean to you? How can you put that into practice?
- God is real, but His ways aren't always "realistic"— meaning, they don't always make sense in this world. How can you live in a way that doesn't make sense to others but is in line with how God wants you to live? What would that look like?

10

WHEN WE'RE FRUSTRATED

One time when I was driving home from college, I was pulled over for speeding. But I got out of the ticket. The cop was nice and said, "You're young; I get you want to be home. Have a safe drive back."

Success!

I was talking to a friend about the incident and pointed out how I had talked my way out of two tickets now. I laughed and said, "I don't know how I get so lucky!"

"I do, Grace," she responded. "You have privilege."

I didn't know what she was talking about. I just got lucky . . . right? What did she mean by "privilege"?

I then started researching more about this topic and realized there was something called "white privilege." I had been ignorant about race relations in our country because I was privileged. Did it affect me? Yes, but I was reaping the benefits from the injustice of this system.

Realizing I lacked education on this topic, I took a class my junior year of college called "Gender, Race, and the Media." This class was offered at my university in our journalism department. It was taught by respected professor Mia Moody-Ramirez.

In this class, I finally learned from different perspectives. I hate that it took a school class to teach me stuff I could have learned a while ago. My class had people from all different sexual orientations, backgrounds, and social classes. I hate to admit this, but my friend group at Baylor University mainly consisted of my sorority sisters. I never tried to make friends in other circles at Baylor. I met people like me and thought that was what life was about—finding friends who are like us.

But through this class I came face-to-face with my privilege. Privilege that came from my background. I also learned more about gender discrimination and experienced moments in which I have faced discrimination as a woman.

I was frustrated with myself for not noticing the injustice in our world.

I was frustrated with our world and nation for having injustice still.

I was frustrated with the bubble I created for myself.

After this class, I asked more questions. I listened to the testimonies of others whose lives were different from mine. My frustration was important. My frustration helped me notice gaps in my own thoughts, learn to speak from the Spirit and not my mind, and most importantly, realize that frustration is not a bad thing. Speaking from the Spirit means to speak with wisdom, self-control, love, and kindness. Speaking our minds causes us to say words that are insensitive, hurtful, and inaccurate. Our minds do not always produce good thoughts; however, the Spirit always leads us to speak God's goodness.

Maybe it's because of my good-girl tendencies, but I always

assumed that frustration was sin. Wasn't it bad to be frustrated? The truth is, sometimes frustration is the first stop to experiencing growth and change. Sometimes frustration comes from the Spirit. Feeling frustrated is not "bad," and being mad is not always a bad thing.

What to Do When We're Frustrated

Don't get me wrong—you should always be patient. You should be patient with others and patient with yourself. But you can be patient and frustrated at the same time. The eleventh chapter of the Gospel of Mark tells a story in which Jesus walked into the temple and discovered merchants using it as a place of business. Jesus drove the animals being sold out of the temple courts and overturned the money changers' tables. He reminded the crowd that the temple was created to be "a house of prayer for all nations," but that they had turned the place into "a den of robbers" (v. 17).

The crowd was amazed at Jesus' actions. He was right, and everyone knew He was. Jesus' outburst also caused the chief priests, teachers, and religious leaders to begin looking for a way to kill him. But the crowd who witnessed Jesus that day learned something important.

Jesus was frustrated. His frustration led to a moment when He called everyone to live a godlier life.

Jesus asks you to love everyone, not to be everyone's best friend. When you become frustrated, follow these three steps.

1. Take a deep breath.

As humans living in a fallen world, our first reaction can sometimes be to sin. Sin is sometimes our first response when we are frustrated, so we must fight against temptation. When you are tempted to speak your mind, go to prayer. Fight the urge to text that long paragraph, to gossip to your peers, and to do the irrational freak-out. Fight the urge to worry about the what-ifs. Go to prayer. Allow your frustration to lead to communication with God.

Let me be clear: I know there may not always be time to take three business days off to pray and reflect on what just happened. I now notice my privilege and know I may not be in the same situations as you. When you're faced with life-threatening situations, you may not be able to step away. However, I firmly believe that if you walk with Jesus daily, you will prepare to find the wisdom on how to handle all frustrations. Be in constant communication with God so He becomes a guide for you.

2. Listen to the Spirit.

Trust the Spirit when it comes to what to do. The Spirit will never tell you to do anything unbiblical. So if what you're doing isn't biblical, your response is coming from your own mind, not from the Spirit.

This incident is trivial compared to what many in our nation are going through, but it taught me an important lesson. Back in high school, a girl tweeted something bad about me. My immediate reaction was to seek her out in the parking lot and call her out on her insecurity. And I did. In the process, I made a comment I still regret: "Do you really think tweeting about me makes you look better?"

My comment was not truth-filled. It came out of my pride and lack of self-control. My comment failed to show her love because it reflected that I was more concerned with making her feel stupid than loved.

Be someone who listens to the Spirit. Read the Bible so you can decipher what is from the Spirit and what is from sin.

When my friend was frustrated with my ignorance, she told me straight to my face that it wasn't luck; it was privilege. I believe her comment and bluntness came from the Spirit. And when I was frustrated with my ignorance, the Spirit led me to take a class on a topic that scared me.

3. Be alert.

I used to deal with frustration in a passive-aggressive way. I would become upset, laugh it off, and then gossip about my feelings. That is not biblical. Tension can be good because it can cause us to process difficult conversations. Now when I am frustrated with someone, I trust the Spirit and I am alert to tell others what God puts on my heart. You never need to apologize for speaking from the Spirit.

To you, my friends who also get frustrated with people who hurt you, use you, or do you wrong, do me a favor and follow those three steps. Stop running away from tension. Tension helps us grow. Just like a workout that hurts and causes you to be sore, sometimes tension hurts. Sometimes it challenges you. But as my gym trainer said, if it doesn't challenge you, then it won't change you.

And to those who fight frustration in heavier ways, it is my prayer that your frustration will lead you to a Spirit-led moment that challenges and changes injustice. And may all others learn from you, stand by you, and listen to your frustration, and may they become frustrated too.

Real Talk

- Describe a time when you became frustrated with something someone did or said. Why did that frustrate you?
- Have you ever been frustrated with yourself? If so, when?
- What does it mean that the Spirit will never call you to something that contradicts the Bible? Can you think of an example?

- Do you tend to be scared of difficult conversations or tension with others? If so, why?
- How can you work toward embracing both the Spirit and the tension that helps you grow?

Part 3

AM I THE ONLY ONE WHO IS STILL SEARCHING FOR MY PURPOSE?

WHEN WE MESS
UP AGAIN

I woke up one morning after a night out. I was in college and had given up alcohol. I was doing better. Then some of my wilder friends told me, "Grace, we miss the old you! Come out with us again just this once!"

They made me feel wanted. I'd been feeling lonely, and being invited by a group felt so good. So I went out with them.

After months of working to grow in my faith, I messed up again. I was twenty-one, so of legal age to drink, but I didn't just casually drink wine with the girls. I drank one too many drinks and blacked out. I tried to blame blacking out on my being a "lightweight" and not eating enough dinner beforehand. But I knew the truth. I knew exactly what I was doing. I drank my insecurities away. There is no worse feeling than waking up wondering, *How did I get home?* I don't recommend it.

I remember being hungover and lying on the cold tile floor of the bathroom, mad at myself. I was mad because I had enjoyed getting drunk before I blacked out. I felt wanted. I felt cool. I woke up to texts and pictures of my friends and me partying, and the pictures did make me laugh at first. But then they made me feel upset and ashamed. I was mad because, yes, I'd made mistakes and sinned. But I'd also had fun doing so.

I had many thoughts after my night out:

Well, I tried.

Maybe obedience is impossible.

Maybe I will never live a full-out life for Jesus.

Should I just admit that sin is more powerful than God? Anyway, obedience would make life lame.

Maybe I can't fulfill God's Word. All I can do is try.

I was wrong—especially with that last thought. I can do more than just try. I can become how God wants me to be. This doesn't create a better me, though—just a more purposeful me.

It's important to understand that God doesn't want a better you. God doesn't want you to hustle and be the best version of yourself that you can create. He wants you to be the you He created you to be. When we try to be better, we are not fixing the problem.

The problem with our sin is that when we go back to our sin, we also have a pride issue. We are saying to God, "I trust this world and myself more than I trust You."

God does not want you to be obedient so that you will give up something, like friends and fun times. He wants you to be obedient so you can gain something even better. He wants you to be with Him.

An Example of Trust and Obedience

Mary was Jesus' mother. The Bible says she was a virgin who became pregnant through the power of the Holy Spirit. Many scholars believe

Mary was twelve to fourteen years old when the angel Gabriel appeared to her. Notice how Luke recorded her reaction to this scandalous news that she would become pregnant—news that would threaten her engagement, might ruin her whole life, and could even result in her being stoned to death:

> In the sixth month of Elizabeth's pregnancy, God sent the angel Gabriel to Nazareth, a town in Galilee, to a virgin pledged to be married to a man named Joseph, a descendant of David. The virgin's name was Mary. The angel went to her and said, "Greetings, you who are highly favored! The Lord is with you."
>
> Mary was greatly troubled at his words and wondered what kind of greeting this might be. But the angel said to her, "Do not be afraid, Mary; you have found favor with God. You will conceive and give birth to a son, and you are to call him Jesus. He will be great and will be called the Son of the Most High. The Lord God will give him the throne of his father David, and he will reign over Jacob's descendants forever; his kingdom will never end."
>
> "How will this be," Mary asked the angel, "since I am a virgin?"
>
> The angel answered, "The Holy Spirit will come on you, and the power of the Most High will overshadow you. So the holy one to be born will be called the Son of God. Even Elizabeth your relative is going to have a child in her old age, and she who was said to be unable to conceive is in her sixth month. For no word from God will ever fail."
>
> "I am the Lord's servant," Mary answered. "May your word to me be fulfilled." Then the angel left her. (Luke 1:26–38)

When the angel told Mary that she would become a pregnant virgin, Mary responded in three ways that revealed her trust and obedience.

1. "How will this be?"

Immediately before this passage, the same angel told a man named Zechariah that he and his wife would bear a child despite their old age. Zechariah's response differed from Mary's; he lacked trust. He asked the angel, "How can I be sure of this? I am an old man and my wife is well along in years" (Luke 1:18). Because of Zechariah's distrust, he was made unable to speak until his wife gave birth to their son, John the Baptist.

Mary's question—"How *will* this be?" (v. 34, emphasis mine)—shows that she trusted that what the angel said would happen. She just wanted to know the game plan. She did not doubt; she just wanted to know her role. She was ready for her part, and she accepted the answer the angel gave her.

When God calls us to be obedient to a calling or command, we need to respond, "How *will*?" instead of "How *can*?" God can do anything. God will supply you with the strength you need for whatever He has called you to do. You can ask for the steps. Feel free to ask for the game plan. Just do not doubt that God can and will do what He says. As the angel said to Mary, "For no word from God will ever fail" (v. 37).

The question is, will you be like Mary and trust Him?

2. "I am the Lord's servant."

Mary realized she was placed on this earth to obey God. She called herself "the Lord's servant" (v. 38). Mary knew her purpose and trusted that her life was meant for more. She had every right to fear death, loneliness, her body changing, and more. But she didn't fear; she obeyed.

We struggle to give up our sinful habits because we do not trust that our lives are really about obeying God. We think we will miss out on life if we obey Him. But Mary knew she would not be missing out on anything purposeful. In fact, she would bear the Savior who would offer eternity to those who put their faith in Him. I would say

Mary's obedience led her to something cooler than mediocre friendships and popularity.

You, too, can fulfill your calling if you respond to God in this way. Stop being afraid of obedience. Instead, choose to celebrate obedience. When you trust God's call and know your role, you will find something greater than what you walked away from.

3. "May your word to me be fulfilled."

Mary asked for the amazing thing the angel said to her to come true and be fulfilled. I ask God for an easy life. I ask God for a white picket fence, a bunch of friends, killer abs (silly, I know), and a cute boy. Mary asked for the virgin pregnancy that could endanger her life to be fulfilled.

Convicting, right?

Mary trusted that God's word was best for everyone. She trusted that a life lived obedient to God was better than a life without Him. And she didn't just swallow this large pill—she prayed for it. She wanted it. She craved the fulfillment of hard tasks.

If Mary could fulfill her purpose with eagerness and trust, maybe I can stop running away from a life that doesn't consist of blacking out, people-pleasing, and kissing random boys. If Mary can be happy for her body becoming the crib of the Savior, maybe I can get over God asking me to follow Him. God has a task for me that is far greater than taking shots and dancing in clubs. This is something to celebrate and be eager about. I should trust that His word is greater, and following Him will not make me miss out on anything. Following His word gives me purpose.

Three Steps for Living in Obedience

You, too, probably have a secret sin you feel convicted about, pray about, but wind up going back to. Maybe it is gossiping, maybe it is lying, maybe it is believing lies about your worth, maybe it is going too far with your boyfriend or speaking ill of your husband. Whatever it is, stop being afraid of obedience. Trust that God will make a way for you. I know that can feel impossible, but Mary provided us with a beautiful, three-step guide for living in obedience:

1. *Trust that it will happen.* If the Lord asked for it, it can happen. If the Lord said it would happen, it will happen.
2. *Know your role.* You are a servant of God, so stop fearing obedience. You aren't missing out on anything. You are finding purpose.
3. *Be eager.* When you fully trust God, you aren't afraid of His will; you are eager for it. You trust that God isn't just going to make it happen; you trust that it is for good.

Real Talk

- Have you ever asked God, "How *can*" instead of "How *will*"? If so, when?
- Which point in this chapter resonated with you the most?
- Is it difficult for you to acknowledge that you are the Lord's servant? Why or why not?
- Is it difficult for you to ask for God's word to be fulfilled in you? Why or why not?
- What is a sin that you struggle to believe God can steer you away from? Why do you believe that?

12

WHEN WE CAN'T GET IT RIGHT

One time in college, I was singing a silly sorority chant that my friend posted on Snapchat. The song included the line, "We're the one who dates the studs." I chanted "Kappa Sigs" after that line because my best friend, Britta, and I thought that the members of Kappa Sigma, a fraternity, were very cute. Someone from another sorority thought I said, "Kappa sucks," talking about their sorority. A member of that sorority taped a note to my dorm room door about how horrible I was. I never found out who taped the note to my door, but I was embarrassed and felt so misunderstood.

One time a girl with blonde hair went to a party at Baylor and made out with a senior guy. This girl was not me. But what was the rumor the next day? That Grace Valentine slept with this senior. Yep, I was frustrated.

One time someone messaged me that I didn't include enough

scripture in my blog posts. Another girl told me I was assuming people knew the Bible and included too much scripture.

There's always a critic. There's always a rumor. Although I wish I could promise you that everyone will only love you and no one will ever talk bad about you, we both know that is not true. There's always someone who has an opinion that basically says you aren't that great.

I used to exhaust myself trying to go to bat against every rumor. After I learned that everyone—at least, it felt like everyone—thought I'd slept with that senior, I sent him an unnecessary message basically saying, "Hey, it wasn't even me who kissed you, so maybe stop this rumor." That message did not help the situation, but I felt better. Sometimes we make the mistake of worrying about our feelings instead of using wisdom. When we allow our feelings to control the situation, we often allow sin to control. Allow wisdom, not feelings, to control your situations.

After that mean note was taped to the door, I became frustrated at the girls in that sorority. I hate to admit this, but I talked negatively about them. I was not always kind. My hurt caused me to sin, and I am not proud of that. How ironic! A sorority thought I talked bad about them and wrote a note on my door, so in response to their note, I chose to be mean and talk about them. Yeah . . . that showed them.

Perhaps the reason we are exhausted and coming up short is because we have our priorities wrong. We have prioritized pleasing over pursuing. We focus on pleasing those who spout their opinions instead of pursuing Jesus.

Pursuing Jesus as Our Priority

We talked about Mary and Martha earlier, and we saw how Mary sat at Jesus' feet and listened to Him teach while Martha busily prepared dinner. There's another story about the sisters that I love because it demonstrates how Mary boldly pursued Jesus. This passage has been convicting for me:

> Six days before the Passover, Jesus came to Bethany, where Lazarus lived, whom Jesus had raised from the dead. Here a dinner was given in Jesus' honor. Martha served, while Lazarus was among those reclining at the table with him. Then Mary took about a pint of pure nard, an expensive perfume; she poured it on Jesus' feet and wiped his feet with her hair. And the house was filled with the fragrance of the perfume.
>
> But one of his disciples, Judas Iscariot, who was later to betray him, objected, "Why wasn't this perfume sold and the money given to the poor? It was worth a year's wages." He did not say this because he cared about the poor but because he was a thief; as keeper of the money bag, he used to help himself to what was put into it.
>
> "Leave her alone," Jesus replied. "It was intended that she should save this perfume for the day of my burial. You will always have the poor among you, but you will not always have me." (John 12:1–8)

There Mary was, worshipping Jesus at His feet and using her expensive perfume to honor Him. She was saying, "Lord, I love You, I pursue You, and I honor You." She was embracing the Lord's presence and was not worried about the financial burden of giving Him her expensive perfume. She was not thinking about tomorrow or being "smart" with her possessions; she was thinking about worshipping Jesus.

One of the disciples, Judas, was known for stealing money. His comment concerning Mary not using the perfume to help the poor did not come from a genuine heart. Judas was trying to nitpick. Jesus knew that. His response to Judas teaches us two things.

1. Jesus will stick up for us when we put Him first. ———

Judas's intentions were to tear Mary down for her act of worship. Jesus responded, "Leave her alone" (v. 7). Jesus stood up for Mary. He will always protect our acts of worship. In a world that says it's a waste of time to give Jesus our priority, He says that He knows what is best. Jesus tells the world He is on our side. When our Savior is on our side, we will stand strong.

2. There will always be more things to do, but time ——— with Jesus is precious.

Jesus responded to Judas, "You will always have the poor among you" (v. 8). In this line, Jesus was giving us an important reminder. This world will always have work and busyness. There will always be more work to finish. There will always be more tests to study for. There will always be people who need help.

We will always have plenty of opportunities to do big things, work hard, and make a name for ourselves. We will always have people to serve. But pursuing Jesus should be our priority.

If we don't worship Jesus with our time, we can't worship Jesus with our acts of service. If we don't sit at His feet and sacrifice our precious time for Him, we will not do big things.

Jesus' response was powerful. But Mary's response was also powerful. Maybe she said something; maybe she didn't. The Bible doesn't tell us. I like to think that Mary didn't clap back at Judas. I like to think her time was so well spent with Jesus that she didn't exhaust herself trying to convince Judas that her actions were theological or right. Instead, she just responded by worshipping Jesus.

The opinion of anyone who is not Jesus should not exhaust you. If people think you are weird for spending your weekend at church, let them. If people think you are weird for leading high schoolers or middle schoolers in a youth group, let them. If people think you are weird because you're living out your faith in college when you used to be the girl who was at frat parties, let them. Their opinions are not worth proving wrong.

Mary continued worshipping Jesus. This moment of intimacy with Jesus was preparing her for something greater than giving thousands of dollars to the poor. I personally believe that those moments at Jesus' feet prepared Mary for something great. These moments of worship before Jesus died helped prepare her for her next steps in ministry after His death. Although we have little evidence of what she did after Jesus died, I believe she did share with others what she learned at His feet. Her worship in Jesus' presence led to her purpose after His death. Her worship led to her legacy. Her worship led to her evangelism. And your worship leads to your evangelism. Yes, you want to do big things, but first sit at your big Savior's feet.

Sit at Jesus' Feet

You and I are never missing out on our purpose if we are at Jesus' feet. In fact, if we don't worship Jesus first, we can't live for Him. How could we live for someone we don't even know? We can't. We need to embrace His presence before we bring His Spirit to others.

Chances are you, too, are dreaming about doing big things. You want to help others, serve, and make an impact. You are ready to stop exhausting yourself by trying to respond to nitpickers. That is great. I pray you tell others about Him. I pray you are able to tangibly serve your community and Creator.

But most of all, I pray that you prioritize Jesus.

If you want to change the world, worship the One who saved the world. If you want a legacy that lasts, trust the One who lives for eternity.

There's so much more to your story. You can't always win. You can't prove yourself right to everyone. You can do all the right things, and someone will still say that what you are doing is wrong. But that argument is not worth your time or energy.

Just worship Jesus. Sit at His feet. Jesus is preparing you for something great.

Real Talk

- What stuck out to you most about Mary in this story?
- Do you have someone like Judas in your life who nit-picks something you feel called to do? What does this person say?
- How can you stop exhausting yourself by listening to others' opinions?
- What are tangible ways you can worship Jesus this week and find time to pursue Him?

13

WHEN WE HAVE REGRETS

I hopped on to Facebook and saw the news. Kyle got married.

I met Kyle (or at least that's what I'll call him here) while in high school. He was a good, kind, caring guy, and I turned him down for a date.

I hadn't thought of him in years. When I saw he'd married, I couldn't help but stalk his wedding photos and think, *What if I hadn't turned down this guy? Would that have been me standing next to him in these wedding photos? Would I be as happy as his new bride looks in her wedding dress?*

When Kyle and I met, he was in the same friend group of a guy I was seeing. When things went south between me and the guy, Kyle reached out and asked if I was okay.

Over a Chick-fil-A lunch Kyle bought, we talked about our faith and trusting God. I will never forget snotty-crying at Chick-fil-A

87

while I talked about how hard the breakup was and how unworthy I felt. Kyle listened to me unload and then said, "Grace, one day you'll be married, and you'll realize this guy was not worth your tears. Until then, though, cry."

Kyle brought me more napkins to blow my gross snot into. He listened, he told me truth, and he encouraged me.

We stayed in contact during my freshman year of college. I would be lying if I said I didn't use Kyle for emotional intimacy. He always was there when I needed him, and we could relate on a spiritual level. When I was home from school, we hung out, and I quickly realized he intended for our hanging out to be a date. I felt awful knowing I had strung him along. I can't say I didn't see this coming. I knew what I was doing, and I'm not proud of that.

But then five years later, I was staring at his wedding photos and asking myself, "What if?"

We live with what-ifs. We idolize what could have been and regret what we did not do. We regret dating the wrong guy and not dating a great one. We regret the words we chose or the pain we caused. We look back, and instead of seeing God at work in our lives, we see the what-ifs.

No Looking Back

When you live with regret and what-ifs, you fail to trust God. Let's discuss two men in the Bible who did not look back on their pasts. Or anyone's past at all.

Saul was known for persecuting Christians. He was on his way to Damascus to persecute more Christians. However, on his way to Damascus Jesus appeared and caused a light from heaven to flash down. Jesus said, "Saul, Saul, why do you persecute me?" (Acts 9:4). Saul asked, "Who are you, Lord?" (Acts 9:5). Jesus responded, "I am

Jesus, whom you are persecuting. . . . Now get up and go into the city, and you will be told what you must do" (Acts 9:5–6).

After the flash, Saul and the men who were with him stood speechless. They heard the sound but did not see anyone talking. Saul realized he was blind when he got up and the men led him to Damascus.

In Damascus, there was a man named Ananias, whom the Lord appeared to in a vision. Ananias was a known follower of Jesus Christ. He knew plenty of people who had been persecuted by Saul before, but the vision from the Lord asked him to do something crazy. The Lord told him to find Saul praying in a certain location and restore his sight. Ananias was confused. He knew Saul was someone who persecuted Christians and it would be dangerous for him to be around Saul. But the Lord said something clear.

"But the Lord said to Ananias, 'Go! This man is my chosen instrument to proclaim my name to the Gentiles and their kings and to the people of Israel. I will show him how much he must suffer for my name'" (Acts 9:15–16).

So what did Ananias do? He went. He approached the man who had persecuted many Christians, prayed over him, and restored his sight just like Jesus said would happen. And after this, Saul became a believer and was an instrument for God.

Saul and Ananias both looked back on their past, and they trusted God more than they exhausted themselves with what-ifs. Let's look at both.

The book of Acts takes place as the church was being built. Saul was a religious leader who persecuted many Christians, including Stephen, because he mistakenly believed he was honoring God by stamping out the "heresy" of Christianity. Acts 7 is Stephen's testimony and the account of his death by stoning.

While Saul was on his way to persecute and kill more Christians, the Lord blinded him and called out to him. Then He instructed Saul to go to Damascus and wait there until told what to do. Saul in that moment listened to the Lord, whose followers he had been persecuting. After Saul's conversion to Christianity, he became known as Paul and joined the disciples in spreading the good news about Jesus. Paul wrote about half of the New Testament books.

Paul didn't look back on his past and ask, "What if I hadn't been as bad?" He never wished for a prettier testimony. He pressed on toward Jesus and eternity with Him. In fact, he wrote in Philippians 3:14, "I press on toward the goal to win the prize for which God has called me heavenward in Christ Jesus." That verse was actually written while Paul was in prison for telling others about Jesus. He pressed on in all situations. Paul pressed forward by looking away from the what-ifs of his past. He had one goal and one goal only: to chase after Jesus and help others do the same.

Ananias also avoided the what-ifs. Ananias knew well of Saul's reputation for persecuting and killing Christians. When Jesus told Ananias to go see the man who had killed his fellow believers, Ananias obeyed. When Ananias heard from the Lord that this man with the horrible past would be His chosen instrument, he believed the word of the Lord. Ananias was not concerned about Saul's reputation; he gave the Lord's words more power than he gave Saul's past.

Like Saul and Ananias, you and I should be people who press on toward Jesus, not people who live in the past.

I learned a good lesson from Kyle about not pushing away the good guys. Seeing his wedding photos reminded me that I want to be with a guy who has a deep faith. I want to look at my husband and know that he's seen my snotty tears and he's okay with them.

Reading this account from Acts also reminds me that God will use my past. When we look back and find ourselves exhausted from our mistakes, regrets, and what-ifs, we aren't listening to God's voice. God's voice called Ananias to help a man who was dangerous. God's voice caused Saul to change his life and purpose. God's voice told both of them not to look back on what had happened, but to press forward to what God wanted to happen.

I don't need to sit here and pout over Facebook because I let a good one get away. I can celebrate that my choices, regardless of whether they seem smart or dumb at the time, are leading me to God's purpose for me.

Listen to Jesus, Not the What-Ifs

I used to be the drunk girl at fraternity parties. It sounds silly, but once I started working for a church, I wondered:

What if that person found out about my past?

What would they think if they knew crop tops and booty shorts used to be my uniform?

What would they say if I told them my Sunday mornings used to consist of hangovers and trying to piece together my scattered memories of the night before?

What would they think if they knew I had the opportunity to date a good, Christian guy but fell for the rich fraternity boy who did nothing but disrespect me?

The older I grow, the more I realize that it should not matter what they think.

If Paul exhausted himself listening to the religious leaders' doubts about his new purpose, he would not have been able to hear God's voice.

If Ananias listened to what seemed safe over what God commanded, Paul would not have been saved.

If you, my friend, listen to your doubts, insecurities, what-ifs, and others' opinions of you, you will also miss out on hearing Jesus' voice.

Press on toward Jesus. Close the Facebook tab. Stop stalking your ex. Stop living with regrets. Stop wondering how life would have been if you hadn't made that mistake or taken that risk. Live life in your present with Jesus. Listen to His voice and drown out the exhausting what-ifs.

Looking back on your life and realizing you missed out is not bad to do if it's only for a minute. You can notice a mistake without tiring yourself by replaying the past. Just don't waste your time playing the what-if saga. Don't live in regret. Instead, walk in wisdom. Walk with confidence that your past is lessons learned, and God is talking to you in your present.

You are smarter today than you were yesterday. You are different because of your mistakes and what-ifs. Don't live in them; learn from them. And press on, friend.

Real Talk

- What is one of your what-ifs?
- Have you ever been exhausted by regret? If so, when?
- Your past can make you wiser. How can you learn from your mistakes and not live in them?
- Write a prayer asking for wisdom. If you want wisdom from the Spirit, pray to receive it. Pray for the ability to discern your past for His glory.

14

WHEN WE ARE
OVERLOOKED

During my friend's engagement party, she let some of us try on her beautiful engagement ring. Each person gushed at how shiny and big the diamond was as she slipped it on her finger before passing the ring to the next person.

The ring finally made its way to me. I was excited to try on a rock more expensive than my net worth. I figured this was the closest I would come to wearing my own engagement ring for a long time.

I slid my friend's ring over the top of my ring finger. But no luck putting it all the way on. So I tried another finger. No luck there, either. Then I downsized to my pinkie finger. Phew! The ring fit one of my fingers! But it was so tight that my pinkie started turning red.

What the heck? My fingers are that fat?

93

Sounds silly, right? But for the next two days, I felt so insecure because of my stupid, fat fingers. I went to the nail salon and assumed the lady doing my nails must have been silently judging me for my fat fingers. I even googled what color I should paint my nails in order to make my fingers look slimmer. (Dark neutrals, in case you're wondering.)

We all have quirks about ourselves that we aren't too fond of, and sometimes the smallest flaw can cause us to feel insecure. We become obsessed with finding ways to cover up our flaw. We compare ourselves to others and write story lines that don't exist.

Because of my thighs, no guy will ever want me.

Because of my mediocre résumé, no employer will ever hire me.

Because of my mistakes, my family will never be proud of me.

I used to pout and think I was being overlooked. The truth is, I was correct. Guys looked at other girls more than me. There were prettier girls and more successful peers. It was exhausting to know that I was being overlooked and underappreciated. I was tired of being everyone's plan B.

I think we have all felt overlooked. We grow up thinking we can be anything, that Prince Charming will sweep us off our feet, and that we will have a happily-ever-after kind of life. We are sure we can get our dream job and believe that people are good at heart. But the older we become, the more we play the comparison game. The more we play the comparison game, the more exhausted we become. Despite what our grandmas say, we learn the truth: not everyone cares about us.

I am not going to sugarcoat the truth: you are not the prettiest, smartest, or best girl. This is a big world, and there is someone out there "better" than you. But you weren't called to be someone else. You are not her. That is something to celebrate, not dread. You might have chubby fingers and some class may be too difficult for you, but God never asked you to chase after anything in this world.

Look to the Interests of Others

I admire the apostle Paul. Let's look at a passage of Scripture he wrote while in prison:

> If you have any encouragement from being united with Christ, if any comfort from his love, if any common sharing in the Spirit, if any tenderness and compassion, then make my joy complete by being like-minded, having the same love, being one in spirit and of one mind. Do nothing out of selfish ambition or vain conceit. Rather, in humility value others above yourselves, not looking to your own interests but each of you to the interests of the others. (Philippians 2:1–4)

When we become frustrated because we feel overlooked, it's because we are living life out of our own vain conceit. We are focused on our own interests. We desire to be seen, wanted, and noticed. Although this is normal, you don't have to remain in that position. You can do what Paul said and look to the interests of others.

You can look at others as community instead of competition. You can focus on connecting instead of competing. When you value others, you cheer them on when they succeed instead of pouting because you aren't as good as they are.

The Problem of Comparison

I remember once when I was going on dates with a guy, and, of course, I searched for any information on his past girlfriends. I don't know why I tortured myself with this hobby, but I did. I stalked one of this guy's exes on social media and discovered that she was a cute, popular, chill, surfer-type girl. Compared to her, I was his dramatic, not-as-pretty-or-smart, half-cool, baby-faced, new girl.

He probably likes her better than me, I told myself.

On our next date, I felt insecure the whole time. I wasn't acting like myself, and I could tell he noticed. That made it even more difficult to act normal! I had allowed my insecurity to creep into my thoughts and affect my actions and my mood. I gave lies more power than God.

When you allow yourself to trust your insecurity over Jesus, you are stating that the cross was not enough. You are giving lies more power than they should have and creating an idol out of titles that come from the world.

I'm not saying this girl wasn't prettier than me. She was! But this guy was going on a date with me, not her. He did not want her; he wanted me.

God wants you. He doesn't want you to conform to vain conceit and value things from this world over Him. If God wanted two of that girl, He would have made two of her. He's God. He can do anything.

But God wants you. He chose you. He brought you this far, and He has a plan for you. Stop denying Him glory by denying your worth.

Others might overlook you, and that's just the way life goes sometimes. But when you look toward the interests of others first and live a life that reflects Him, you won't care about receiving attention from others. You won't place as much importance on success. And I am a true believer that when you stop finding your worth in titles, success will come to you.

When you carry the Spirit in your heart and value others, people won't overlook you because they won't be able to help but notice that you're different. That you love differently. That you live differently. That you don't get caught up in what others think about you.

When Jesus loved people radically, crowds talked about Him. Jesus never loved others so He could attract attention, but crowds couldn't help but pay attention to Him. If you stop exhausting yourself with people-pleasing and attention-seeking, you can live a life that creates a beautiful legacy. Everywhere you go will be left better not because you were there, but because the Spirit was there through you.

As long as we're living in this world, we will deal with the tension of wanting to be like this world. When we crave something from the world and compare ourselves to those around us, we will feel the tension that comes from living in a temporary world where nothing can satisfy us.

Others First

Perhaps you feel overlooked because you aren't looking toward the One who did choose you and does love you despite your flaws. When you face this tension, don't run from it and slap on some "I'm fine," quick-fix bandage. When you face this tension, dig deep into your heart and ask yourself, "Why do I think something from this world matters more than the cross?"

On days when I struggle with being overlooked, I pull out my journal and write down three truths. My three truths usually go something like this:

1. *I take the hard pill to swallow—and swallow it.* Maybe she is prettier or more successful than I am. I write down my biggest fear that could very well be true. I write a kind word about whoever appears to be more than me.
2. *I write that it does not matter.* I write the truth that God loves me as I am, and I don't need to worry about being seen and admired in this world.
3. *I write, "God isn't finished with me yet."* I have room to grow because God is still at work in me. I need to stop being hard on

myself for not doing things in my time or in my way because God is at work creating a more beautiful story with my life than I could ever imagine.

Next time you feel overlooked, do yourself a favor and remind yourself, "Others first." That other girl's apparent success does not mean you failed. Her beauty does not mean you are ugly. Her great life does not mean God is not using your life for His glory.

God wants you. And anyone who overlooks a Spirit-lived life is missing out. Focus on living for Him, and you will no longer be exhausted by the need for attention.

Real Talk

- Have you felt overlooked? When and why?
- Read Philippians 2:1–4 again. Does the fact that Paul wrote this while in prison add any meaning to this passage for you? If so, what?
- How does Philippians 2:1–4 relate to the life you desire to live?
- What are three ways you can focus on Christ instead of the world?
- Write your version of the three truths I write in my journal when I struggle with being overlooked.

15

WHEN WE TRY TO
BE SOMEONE ELSE

Not long ago I spoke at a college where a guy I went on a date with had graduated from. When I say one date, I mean I had a crush on the guy, and it felt too good to be true that he asked me for a date. What kind of dream was this? But after two and a half hours of talking over coffee—I don't even like coffee—he never texted me again. So that was the end of our story. Cute, right?

When I was asked to speak to a group at his alma mater, I reached out to him to find out more information about the group. He was kind and helpful. He gave me insider information about the size of the group and the type of students I'd be speaking to. He even offered— insisted, actually—to find a place for me to stay with some girls who were his friends. He was no longer in that area, but he said his friends lived close to the venue and it would be fun for everyone involved if I stayed the night there instead of driving back home.

I thanked him but said I would prefer to return home after the event.

Then I found out the event would start late. How "college," right?

My bedtime post-grad was 10:00 p.m., so I would definitely need to stay at his friends' house. I got back in touch with him and asked if he could connect me with the girls.

"Yeah!" he replied. "Her name is Haley [or at least I'll call her that for this story]. She's actually my girlfriend. She would love to have you."

His girlfriend? Of course!

My reaching out to him was not flirting. (I keep telling myself that.) I had valid questions that I knew he could answer. But I felt stuck after saying I needed a place to stay. I had two options:

1. I could stay at the house of the girlfriend of the guy I liked more than I should have after one coffee date. I would probably feel awkward right before a big speaking gig. I would probably stare at his girlfriend and catch myself thinking about how great she was compared to me. I mean, she probably even made her bed every morning! And I bet she cooked actual food instead of eating Chick-fil-A four times a week. Sounds like a fun visit, right?

2. I could say, "Just kidding. I'm good. I don't need a place to stay after all." But then I would risk looking like a girl who felt uncomfortable staying with the girlfriend of a guy I went on one coffee date with. Which *was* how I felt. But I wouldn't be seen as the cool, chill girl if I avoided staying at her place. Would he possibly think I liked him if I didn't stay at his girlfriend's?

What did I do? I sucked it up, felt uncomfortable, and stayed with his girlfriend. She was nice, kind, and even had a whole package of goodies waiting for me when I arrived. Honestly, if we had gone to the same college, we probably would have been friends. Or I would have wanted a friend like her. I took a nap on her bed and did my makeup in her bathroom.

I was such a chill girl—externally. Internally, I was far from chill.

I laugh at my own story because I do stuff like this all the time. I do stuff I don't want to do, and I do it because I want other girls and guys to think I am chill. I want to be one of the cool girls who can drink beers with the boys and watch every sports game. I don't want to be one of those wild girls like on *The Bachelor*.

But the truth is, I'm a *Bachelor*-watching, cheap-white-wine-sipping, not-chill girl. Even in my twenties, I have crushes on boys who don't know I exist. I overreact, and I'm sensitive. I'm not chill. But I am Grace Valentine. Perhaps that's my charm.

Whether you are a chill girl and don't often show emotions or you wear waterproof mascara every day like me just in case you cry, we have all tried to be someone we are not. We have all found ourselves exhausted from trying to save face. We have all become overwhelmed with living a life others admire instead of a life God admires.

Stop Trying to Be Someone You're Not

When we spend our days trying to convince people to like us, we don't have any time to chase after Jesus. What a shame it would be to get to the end of this all and stand before a God we haven't heard, all because we were too busy convincing people to like us.

Stop trying to be someone you are not.

Here's a passage from Psalms that I find helpful truth in:

> You made me; you created me.
> Now give me the sense to follow your commands.

> May all who fear you find in me a cause for joy,
>   for I have put my hope in your word.
>
> Psalm 119:73–74 NLT

We can learn three things from this passage about what to do when we are tempted to try to be someone we're not.

1. Remember that God created you.

God took the time to make each of us unique. What an insult it would be if we spent our days insulting His work by trying to be someone else.

I love that this passage starts with, "You made me; you created me" (v. 73 NLT). It's easy to depersonalize the Bible. We say God created everyone! That is true, but don't forget that God created *you*, the individual. He created you uniquely. He was not in a rush when He planned you. He was purposeful.

Don't you dare become someone other than the person He made. On the difficult days when you wish you were different, remind yourself that God made *you*.

2. Pray for wisdom.

This psalm says, "Now give me the sense to follow your commands" (v. 73 NLT).

Have you ever done anything stupid? If you are anything like me, you've done stupid things probably more than you would like to admit. I often forget to use my common sense. I make life more difficult than it has to be. And in those moments, I realize that I have forgotten to pray for wisdom. I need to talk to God honestly.

Don't just ask God for things. Don't just ask Him for what you want. Ask Him for self-control. Ask Him to help you choose to follow His commandments. I promise you, God desires for you to want to live out His truth. Ask Him for a clear route, and He will give it to you. It might not be easy, but you will be filled with the Spirit, and living for Him will not be so hard.

3. Put your hope in His Word. ────────────────────

When I board a plane, I might not see the pilot, but I trust he's in the cockpit and will safely take me to my destination. In the same way, I might not always see God Himself, but I have His Word, and I need to put all my hope and faith in His Word. I need to trust that His Word is true, is right, and is worthy of my trust in my everyday life. I will not become tired of who I am if I know who He is. And it is easier to know who He is if I'm hanging out with Him.

Hang out with Him by reading His Word. Putting hope in His Word also means that anything from this world doesn't matter. His Word is true. Anything that does not reflect His Word is a distraction.

Trust God's Design for You

It is easy to want to be someone else. It is normal to think you need to become something you are not. But God does not want you to be normal. He wants you to live according to the hope from His Word. His Word says you are made by Him. "You created my inmost being; you knit me together in my mother's womb. I praise you because I am fearfully and wonderfully made" (Psalm 139:13–14). Live with that truth.

You are allowed to have feelings. You do not have to be the chill girl. You also are allowed to be the bro. But you are wanted as you are. Stop hiding who God made you to be. Don't get me wrong: I hope you don't overthink sleeping on a random girl's pullout couch because she dates a guy you like. But I also hope you listen to what makes you tick. You can say no. You can say yes. But be you.

You are made in God's image. Stop wasting your time trying to be someone else. What a shame it would be if you left this earth without getting to know the you God created you to be. Live your faith. Live by His Word. But stop trying to be someone else.

The first step to trusting God is trusting that He made you the way you are for a reason. Start there.

Real Talk

- Have you ever tried to be someone you're not? Did this lead to an uncomfortable situation? If so, what happened?
- Which point in Psalm 119:73–74 resonated with you the most?
- Is it difficult for you to trust that God made you who you are for a reason?
- What is one step you can take in order to trust that you are who you are for a reason?

Part 4

AM I THE ONLY ONE STRUGGLING TO TRUST THAT GOD IS THERE?

16

WHEN GOD
IS SILENT

"Don't you just love when Jesus whispers into our sweet, sweet hearts?"

A girl at my university said that in a chapter meeting for my sorority. I remember laughing inside. *He "whispers into our hearts"? What does that even mean?*

I used to become so frustrated when Christians used weird phrases to talk about God speaking to them. I was frustrated for two reasons:

1. *The language they used was misleading.* They used pretty words, but did they mean them? Did they hear an audible whisper? How did that whisper go toward their hearts? Why were their hearts so "sweet"?

2. *I was jealous that other people heard Jesus and I didn't.*
   Because I couldn't feel or hear Jesus at the time, I was rather
   annoyed that He was apparently sharing His voice with other
   people, including my sorority sister. Why was Jesus talking to
   her and not to me?

If you are like me and relate to the feelings of confusion or jealousy that come when you hear others talk about Jesus talking to them,
this chapter is for you.

I want to assure you that it's okay to struggle with this topic.
It's okay to be a Christian and experience times when you wonder where God is. It's okay not to be a Christian and be skeptical
about God.

But while it is okay to experience doubt (in fact, it's normal!)—
and I don't want you to be ashamed for struggling with it—you will
miss out on true faith if you stay in your doubt.

Don't feel guilty for doubting, but also don't get stuck in your
doubt. Faith is stronger than any question you have. Jesus is bigger
than any of your doubts. There is hope. By reading this chapter, you
are showing that you are willing to listen to Him and desire to hear
from Him.

Hearing God in the Silence

I used to crave desperately for Jesus to speak to me. Wouldn't it be
easier if He just proved to me He was there by talking to me audibly?
But I've learned in this process that I've complicated His voice. And
I've not given Him an opportunity to speak.

During spring 2019, I decided to run a half marathon in the
mountains of North Carolina. I made this decision a month before
the race. A half marathon is a little over thirteen miles, and at that

point, I could run about two miles, max. I hadn't trained much, but I had a bundle of eagerness and a good friend named Anna who would be running as well. What else could I need? No one could stop me!

Embarrassing confession: I am awful with technology. The night before the race, I was trying to figure out Spotify, Pandora, and how to download podcasts. I had no trouble finding and playing songs and podcasts on my phone when I needed to, and I was accustomed to listening to music through YouTube. But I needed to download everything that I wanted to listen to during the race.

The next morning I woke up early and followed all the pre-race tips Anna had given me. I ate half a banana and did my stretches. I was ready. I hadn't trained well, but I kept telling myself that running is more of a mental thing.

Until mile three, I was feeling good and listening to my favorite *The Bachelor* podcasts. That's when I completed the first big loop and began running downhill through a trail that had the most beautiful view of the mountains. On that trail, my podcast stopped playing. I tried to turn on YouTube and Pandora. Neither of those played, either. Huffing and puffing while I ran, I tried to figure out what had happened.

I had lost reception on my phone because of my location in the mountains.

No music. No way to listen to my podcasts.

I went to my downloads. Nothing there. I had messed up my download the night before.

But I did see one song on my iCloud from a while back, "The A Team" by Ed Sheeran. That song was great in 2011. But it was a folk ballad, and really not the best vibe for running the next ten miles.

Normally, I would panic at the threat of two hours of silence. Silence has never been my friend. When I'm in an elevator with a stranger, I tell her I like her shoes. I can't bear a minute of awkward silence. When the Uber driver picks me up and I'm alone, I ask something like, "How long have you been Ubering?" Does my driver want to talk to me? Probably not. But I feel awkward sitting in silence.

For some reason that morning, I laughed, looked at the mountains, and thought, *Well, God, You're gonna have to talk to me today.*

The funny thing is that before the half marathon, I was complaining to a friend about how it seemed like God wasn't speaking to me. I had been asking myself questions like, "Why can't God just talk to me and tell me what He wants from me? Why can't He assure me that life is going to be okay?" I was praying lots and writing out my prayers, but I felt like I wasn't getting even a simple hello from God in return.

I've felt that way countless times.

When I was seventeen and going through my first heartbreak, I asked God, "Why?" I assumed He never answered.

When I was nineteen and blacking out at frat parties, I asked God to give me a way out. But there was no clear, deep voice telling me what to do.

When I was twenty-two and in post-grad world, I asked God to tell me why I had been single for so long. He didn't make a great boy appear out of thin air.

During the duration of that half marathon without reception, music, and podcasts, I learned that silence isn't scary after all. As I ran in silence, I felt God. I didn't hear an audible, deep voice telling me my future. But I felt peace. I felt God telling me that He had me. And the coolest part? The trail I was running was the same trail I had ridden mountain bikes on at sixteen while asking God to give me purpose. Now here I was, six years later, laughing at myself because I wouldn't have reflected on those times if not for the lost reception and my inability to download music correctly.

Two Things to Do When
You Can't Hear God
——————

If you don't believe you can hear God, here are two things I hope you
will do.

1. Be silent and be still. ————————————————

Stop thinking so much. Stop trying to control the conversation
with God all the time. Sit in stillness, take a deep breath, and allow
God to control the conversation with you.

I love the part of Psalm 46:10 that simply says, "Be still, and know
that I am God." When I talk with students in my church's youth group
who are overwhelmed with anxiety, life, and difficult situations, I
instruct them to breathe in and say, "Be still." Then when they breathe
out, they say, "and know that I am God."

I've observed that that verse calms panic attacks, calms frustrated
teens, and helps the nervous middle school worship leader be reminded
of truth before she takes the stage to lead our group.

Being still isn't only about being physically still. It means slow-
ing down your mind from all the what-ifs and any other distraction
from Jesus. It means stopping your mind from racing twenty million
different directions.

Being still means focusing on God's strength.

2. Stop expecting God to speak the way you wish He ——
would.

God's voice isn't a literal whisper. Well, maybe He does do that
for some people. But to me, His voice is found in the tugs in my soul
that push me to do something out of the ordinary for me. His voice is
found in my life situations.

I stopped believing in coincidences the minute Jesus entered my heart. I learned that when you have a Savior who can move mountains, He is the One who causes the "coincidences" to happen.

There's no such thing as "chance." That's Jesus.

Recognizing Jesus in the Storm

Matthew, Mark, and Luke gave accounts of a time when the disciples were in a boat without Jesus and a bad storm came upon them. The disciples had just witnessed Jesus miraculously feeding more than five thousand people with only five loaves of bread and two fish. When they saw a dark figure walking on water during the storm, they didn't recognize that it was Jesus. Instead, they yelled, "It's a ghost" (Matthew 14:26).

When I first read this story, I thought, *Really, guys?*

The disciples had seen firsthand how Jesus performed miracles. And they had just been part of a really amazing one. But when they were caught on the water in a storm, all of a sudden a ghost appearing to them seemed more probable than Jesus.

However, after reading that story, I felt convicted. I do the same thing the disciples did.

I've seen Jesus do some pretty amazing things. He's made a way when there was no way. He has healed me from my heartbreaks and delivered me from my worst. He has guided me to where I am now, and He has led me to who I have become. He has worked in my life. I haven't heard a deep voice or seen a burning bush, but my life is evidence that Someone has my back and that Someone is catching me when I fall.

Yet, I still doubt.

I fail to see Jesus because I'm too busy assuming it isn't Him. He could be walking on water right in front of me, but because I am living with doubt, not faith, I don't recognize Him. I call His work in my life a "coincidence" or just "chance."

I think there's a reason Jesus isn't running around in a white robe bibbidi-bobbidi-booing everywhere. There's a reason He came as a poor servant instead of a rich king. There's a reason He wore a crown of thorns and was mocked and abused instead of wearing a golden crown and being widely worshipped while on this earth. There's a reason that, in the storm, He was on top of the crashing waves, walking with confidence—but the disciples didn't recognize Him and could only see a dark figure.

Jesus Isn't Hiding from You

Jesus wants us to find Him in the chaos.

He is still there. He isn't hiding from you. He's just waiting for you and me to open our eyes. He is waiting for us to remove the doubt from our lenses and see Him for who He is—a Savior who loves us and who doesn't need human language to communicate with us.

We serve a Jesus who can walk on water, move mountains, and make the sun rise. It would be boring if He used His voice instead of using life situations to speak to us.

So, how do we hear God?

We hear Him in the quiet moments we experience while reading His Word. We hear Him in the silence. We hear Him when we finally pray as if being in His arms is more important than being anywhere else. When we finally stop our racing thoughts and focus on Him, we can feel and hear His presence.

We hear Him with every rejection, knowing that is His protection. We see Him with every sunrise and in rainbows. We see Him through every friend who has had arms open to hug us when we needed it.

If we look for Him, we can see God every day.

He may not come how we prefer.

He may not come how we expect.

But He's there. And on the days we can't feel Him, we must not be praying or noticing Him. It is our problem, not His.

To you, my friend, who struggles to hear and feel God, drop your expectations. Pray right now and stop praying like you have somewhere more important to be. Stop putting time constraints on God and let Him control the conversation. Stop being scared of silence and give Him the opportunity to speak to you through His Word, through truth that enters your thoughts and your life.

Open your eyes today and see Him in the little things. Yes, He is a mystery, but He's a beautiful mystery I know to be true. And He's a beautiful mystery I believe you, too, know is greater than your doubts.

Real Talk

- Read the story of the disciples in the boat from Matthew 14:22–33. Note verse 26, where the disciples cried out in fear, "It's a ghost." Have you ever said, "It's a coincidence," when actually God was doing something in your life? If so, when?
- In what ways do you hear God speak in your everyday life?
- Is it difficult for you to be still physically and in your thoughts? Why or why not?
- Write a prayer, and then give God a chance to speak. Do not rush this. Be still and silent, and listen for God.

17

WHEN CHRISTIANS ARE LAME

One of my friends recently got married. She told me about a young girl who felt bad dancing at her wedding because she thought God doesn't want people to dance. Every song that came on would stress her out. She didn't know how to have fun at the wedding because everything she did she felt bad about.

I laughed at the story. My friend laughed. Then I became concerned: *Is this what people think Christianity is supposed to be like?*

I doubt that young girl at the wedding is the only one who thinks a Christian is called to sit still, look pretty, and pretend to have it all together. *Your Bible has to be highlighted, and your reputation has to be pristine. And don't you dare jump around to any song by Drake! No dancing, no jumping, no smiling!*

When did Christians become so dang lame?

Truth be told, I'm over lame Christians.

I know that sounds aggressive, but Jesus never asked Christians to be lame. In fact, I do not think Jesus wants His followers sitting in a corner having a theological debate about song choices. I think Jesus would prefer that His followers make friends with everyone, eat some good food at the table with people from all walks of life, and celebrate.

Here's the deal: if dancing causes you to sin, then don't dance. But the truth is, I am a firm believer that Jesus called us to the opposite of a lame life. Jesus called us to a life of adventure and being a light in the room.

Being obedient does not mean you have to be lame.

A Life-Changing Encounter

One of my favorite passages in the Bible involves a group of men who had a friend who was unable to move. They desperately wanted to get to Jesus because they knew He could heal their friend. So, what did they do? They waited in line and followed the rules and slowly approached Jesus.

Just kidding! That would be typical.

These men were chasing after Jesus with full faith, so they did something atypical. They climbed onto the roof, made a hole, and lowered their friend down to Jesus. Their friend was healed, and his sins were forgiven.

Look at what happened:

One day Jesus was teaching, and Pharisees and teachers of the law were sitting there. They had come from every village of Galilee and from Judea and Jerusalem. And the power of the Lord was with Jesus to heal the sick. Some men came carrying a paralyzed man on a mat and tried to take him into the house to lay him before Jesus.

When they could not find a way to do this because of the crowd, they went up on the roof and lowered him on his mat through the tiles into the middle of the crowd, right in front of Jesus.

When Jesus saw their faith, he said, "Friend, your sins are forgiven." (Luke 5:17–20)

I notice three important things in this passage.

1. The religious law-keepers were sitting by Jesus. ——

These religious leaders were sitting by Jesus. But Jesus noticed the faith of the other men who were not sitting by Him. So often we think going to church and going through the motions is what Jesus wants. But Jesus does not want your attendance; He wants your faith. He wants your adventure. He wants your love and your willingness to step out in faith. It is important that we sit still and know that He is God, but when we know who Jesus is, we will then desire to share Him. Were the religious law-keepers doing the normal thing? Probably. But in this moment what Jesus noticed was the faith of the men who brought their friend through the roof.

It is important to know that Jesus wants your stillness and wants you at His feet because He wants your heart. When He has your heart, you will also do crazy things on occasion. Sometimes that means you'll sit at His feet while everyone is busy hustling and studying and working their lives away. Sometimes that means your day will be focused on bringing your friends to Jesus. Embrace the adventure that comes with both. Sit still when you are resting in Jesus' name, but also be the one who jumps onto a roof to help someone who needs Jesus.

2. The men cared more about healing their friend —— than being normal.

If we want to be Christians who change this world, we can't settle for being normal. We are going to have to go through walls. We are going to have to make helping our friends more important to us than what religious leaders think about us.

I hope most religious leaders today understand the importance of having friends from different walks of life. But I have personally seen some Christians—and sadly, I've been one—who felt that engaging in theological debates at church with fellow Christians was more important than celebrating a wedding on a dance floor with nonbelievers.

Do not condone the sins of others, but also don't keep your distance from them. Even if they are living sinful lives and need healing from Jesus, just sitting in a corner distancing yourself from anything worldly will not save them. Grab your friend, and bring her to Jesus. Stop waiting for your friend to get up on Sunday morning and decide she will try out church. Bring her to Jesus. Bring her just the way she is. Jesus' blood is more powerful than any situation. Act like it.

3. When Jesus saw the men's faith, He healed their —— friend's sin.

Notice that Jesus first healed the lame man's sins. Jesus would go on to heal the man's physical body, but Jesus thought the man's spirit was first and foremost what needed immediate healing.

Also, notice that this passage uses the word *their*—"their faith" saved the lame man. It was not the faith of the man who was sick but the faith of his friends that caught Jesus' attention. Your faith in Jesus' healing can lead others to have life-changing encounters with the Spirit.

Anything but Lame

Let's see what happened next in the story:

> The Pharisees and the teachers of the law began thinking to themselves, "Who is this fellow who speaks blasphemy? Who can forgive sins but God alone?"

Jesus knew what they were thinking and asked, "Why are you thinking these things in your hearts? Which is easier: to say, 'Your sins are forgiven,' or to say, 'Get up and walk'? But I want you to know that the Son of Man has authority on earth to forgive sins." So he said to the paralyzed man, "I tell you, get up, take your mat and go home." Immediately he stood up in front of them, took what he had been lying on and went home praising God. Everyone was amazed and gave praise to God. They were filled with awe and said, "We have seen remarkable things today." (Luke 5:21–26)

I notice here three more things.

1. Jesus knew the religious leaders' thoughts.

The fact that Jesus could read people's thoughts shows His power. He immediately responded to the religious leaders' thoughts by talking about how the Son of Man had the authority to forgive sins. This was Him proclaiming His power.

2. Jesus healed the man.

Jesus instructed the lame man to take the mat he once lay on and go home. The man "went home praising God" (v. 25). When we are healed, we are called to go home and bring our praises and good news of Jesus back to where we started. This does not necessarily mean we have to go back to a physical location. But we are each called to take our mat and bring the gospel back to those we know. Jesus did not tell the healed man, "Stay here for the rest of the service." Instead, He told him, "Take your mat and go home" (v. 24). I hope you go to church regularly, but I also hope you go home and praise Jesus to those who don't know Him.

3. The crowd praised Jesus after the friend was healed.

When you help your friends and bring them to Jesus, you aren't changing just them. Others are watching. Others are noticing someone's life change. This life change becomes contagious.

I used to think Christianity was about trying to be perfect, sitting still, following all the rules, and not dancing. I used to be the religious leader who questioned how Jesus could truly forgive *some people's* sins. I sat on the front row, judged people, and questioned God. Then when I struggled to choose Jesus, it was because I was tired of being a lame Christian and seeing lame Christians. I was scared to be obedient to Jesus because I thought it would be lame. I knew some lame Christians, and I didn't want to live like them. I wanted to dance at people's weddings, and I wanted to have a life of adventure.

But when I fell head over heels for Jesus, I realized that our lives are filled with more adventure when we follow the One who gave us life. When we dance with Jesus and follow His lead step by step, we not only create something beautiful; we create something fun. Something that makes the distractions of the world seem lame.

Being a Christian sometimes means taking others through the roof, and sometimes it means being healed publicly and singing praises on our way home while holding our mat. This is anything but lame. Perhaps we as Christians should spend more time carving holes in walls to get people to Jesus. That sounds more fun than sitting still. I'm not saying you have to be the one dropping it low at the wedding, but never, ever think following Jesus means you have to miss out on joy and adventure.

Now, there are some things Christians do that the world calls lame. Like waiting for sex until marriage and not being the one dancing at a bar while taking ten shots. But having been someone who, like many others, has struggled with desiring the things of this world, I can promise you one thing: Jesus' will for you is better than your temporary desires. Jesus' will is not lame because it leads you to His goodness. When you trust that His will is good, you will see that His will is life-giving. The Christian life is not about exhausting yourself with rules; it is about finding life and trust in who He is. And following His lead creates a more adventurous life than the ones you see in the world.

Obedience is not easy. But when you obey your Savior, you will have a joy-filled life. Obeying Him won't always be easy. But it will be worth it because obedience leads to adventure. Obedience leads to climbing onto roofs for those you love and dancing with your sweet Savior.

Let Jesus take the lead, and don't be afraid of dancing at weddings. You do you, but never think following Jesus means you have to miss out on adventure. I'm a firm believer that the greatest adventure is falling in love with your First Love. Falling in love with Jesus will bring you a whole lot of joy.

And if you ever invite me to your wedding, I'll probably be the first on the dance floor. Who needs a plus-one?

Real Talk

- Have you ever thought Christians are lame? Why or why not?
- When you think about obedience to God, how does that make you feel?
- How can you share the gospel in an adventurous way? How would this attract the crowd of unbelievers around you?

18

WHEN WE LET GO OF OUR NEED TO BE RIGHT

"Can I speak to the manager?"

I know what you're thinking: I overheard some middle-aged woman with a short haircut named Susan saying that. She must have been upset because she asked for the salad dressing on the side and the waiter forgot. So now she was throwing a fit trying to get the manager to take her half-eaten salad off her bill.

Nope. Those were my words. I was on the phone with the car shop. I had been involved in a wreck that was my fault. The car shop had pushed back the date my car was supposed to be ready four times already. They had given me the wrong times and failed to call me to make me aware of their mistakes. Now I was calling them to receive an update. And their update was useless because it provided me with no valuable information about when my car would be ready.

Even though my car had suffered only slight damage to the front end, it had been in the shop for over a month—and I had to pay for a rental car the entire time.

The manager and I had a sassy phone conversation.

She said, "I'm sorry—everyone makes mistakes. Haven't you made a mistake?"

I tried to explain that because of the rental car, I was the one paying for their mistake.

Finally, she offered to pay for the final four days of my car rental and said that my car would be ready the next week. She ended the conversation with, "I hope you're happy now."

Well, then!

I was not happy. A fun fact about me is that even though I am an adult, I still cry when an adult raises her voice to me. That conversation turned me into a fifth grader who feared her teacher.

Later, when the dust had settled, I reflected on our phone call.

Was I right? Yes!

But was I kind? No. (And that was a sheepish no.)

We live in a society that often says it is better to be right than to be kind. The problem with being human, though, is that "right" is a state of mind. When two people are in a dispute, one person can be right, but so can the other—in their minds, anyway.

Both the manager and I were convinced we were right. What makes for kindness, however, is usually much less in dispute.

When I look at Jesus, I see Someone who always had the right answer but did not always seek to make it known that He was right. Instead of acting out of frustration and becoming overwhelmed, He acted out of love. Jesus was kind. Jesus was love. And to Him, it was more important to reflect God's love than it was to prove that He was right.

We all have had bad days and taken them out on someone who did nothing wrong. We've all felt justified anger. We've had fair feelings. But when you live with a gentle spirit, you realize that walking in love is more important than proving you are right.

With Jesus, you have nothing to prove. With Jesus, you trust that He is always right and that when you live with Him, you live in truth. That not only is better—it's also a legacy worth living.

Eight Things to Be Instead of "Right"

Here are eight things you and I can strive to be instead of being right. My prayer is that we all will work toward living out these characteristics instead of seeking to prove ourselves.

1. Kind

Jesus told the parable of the good Samaritan in Luke 10:25–37. A man was attacked by robbers and left injured beside a road. A priest walked by, and even though he was religious, he did not help the man. After the priest walked by and did nothing, a second traveler walked by and also ignored the injured man. That man was a Levite, an assistant to the priests in the Jewish temple. Finally, a Samaritan man came and not only took care of the injured man's wounds but also took him to an inn and paid for the remainder of his care.

Samaritans were half-Jewish and half-Gentile (non-Jew). In Jesus' day, Jews despised Samaritans, partly because they believed the Samaritans' religious beliefs made them half-pagan. Of the three travelers who came upon the wounded man in Jesus' parable, the Samaritan was the one who would not be considered "religious" according to the Jews of that time. Yet it was the Samaritan—not the two who were considered faithful because of their religious duties—who stopped to help the wounded man.

Jesus told this parable to point out to the crowd that having a religious background isn't important. Loving your neighbor is.

Live a kind life. See the hurt in others. Allow them to see the love of God in how you love them. Aim to be known as a kind person rather than a person who has to prove herself right.

2. Loving

God is love. When we live with God in our hearts, we reflect His love to all we meet. Love doesn't care about worldly titles. Love doesn't care about accuracy. Love will always find a way to care for people, no matter the cost.

When Jesus died on the cross for us, He exemplified true love. Our lives are meant to look like Jesus'. I would rather live a life that loves boldly than a life that wins the contest for being "right." It is more important to stretch out our arms to others than it is to be right.

A loving life is a life that's worth living.

3. Someone who gets walked on

I used to say, "There's no worse feeling than being walked on." I always wanted to be right because I believed that being right protected me. But in those moments, I was speaking from my trust issues and not trusting Jesus.

Jesus was not merely walked on—He was trampled on. He was spit on. He gave up everything for us. Stop fearing being walked on. Being walked on by others is often a price we pay for living a life of love. Expect it. Be more afraid to live a prideful life than to be "too kind."

Before I go on, let me be clear: abuse is never okay, and if you are being emotionally or physically abused, you need to walk away. When I say "walked on," I am not referring to abuse. There's a difference between someone taking advantage of your kindness and someone putting you in a harmful situation. Please know the difference, and if you think you are being abused, reach out for help.

Let me give you an example of what I mean by someone taking advantage of your kindness. Over the years, I have led many students from all walks of life. Some are from the summer camp I worked for in college, some are from small groups and Bible studies I have led, and others are peers or younger girls from school with whom I just decided, *Maybe we can talk about Jesus together.* Most of these relationships are fun and make me smile and always see goodness. I see world changers in their faces. But I remember a time when one of these students "walked on" me. She got pregnant and made the decision to walk with Jesus. I was so happy for her and her sweet baby, and I did a lot to help her. However, she never had this immediate, radical transformation I expected. How silly, right? I expected her transformation to look the way I wanted it to look and didn't trust God to be at work in her heart. In my disappointment, I wrongly made her faith all about me, and I now know that. But the truth was, sometimes I felt used by our relationship. I was always there for her, but she never seemed to want to listen to anything I had to say. And although I'm sure this was not her intention, it made me sad.

I told a friend about my efforts with my student and how the student made me feel. My friend responded with wisdom: "So what if you're being used? You get a chance to preach the gospel. Even if she isn't responding how you desire, God gave you the opportunity to show her love."

After this conversation with my friend, I stopped waiting for results and began celebrating my opportunities with anyone who may take advantage of my kindness. I might be getting walked on. I might not always see the results I desire or expect, but I always see Jesus. I always see the beauty that comes from living for Him. I have Jesus, and I have love from His Spirit. That is more important than results and being "right."

4. Gentle

Gentle was my word of the year for 2020 because being gentle is so dang hard for me. I am aggressive by nature. I speak my mind more often than I should. If it is not already obvious, you can guess that I am all about girl power. It is such a shame that women's voices have been silenced for years. We naturally raise girls to be quiet and look pretty, and many women struggle to find their voices because of this. So let me be clear: speaking up is not the issue. I do not believe you can speak up too much. I hope every woman reading this finds her unique voice and speaks up. However, when I say I spoke my mind more than I should, it means I prioritized my feelings above the gospel. The mind is a powerful thing, but it is also an individual thing. I sometimes spoke my feelings before thinking of others or the gospel as a whole.

I hope to always speak up with love in mind. I hope my frustration is based on Scripture, and I hope I use my squeaky, high-pitched voice to stand against injustice, love the hurt, and spread Jesus' name. However, I hope I do so with gentleness in mind, not selfishness. Jesus was gentle. Every word He used served a purpose. He looked people in the eyes with kindness before He guided them to live a different life. Jesus was gentle to the hurt and empathetic to the sinner.

I knew a girl who said she wanted to stop sleeping with random guys. She told me that often, but then Friday night would come, and she would sleep with another guy. I spent so much time holding her accountable and trying to make her understand that what she was doing was a sin that I forgot to be gentle with her.

One day as I prayed for gentleness, I realized that I hadn't asked my friend why she was sleeping with random guys.

The next time we had lunch together, I was purposely different toward her. Instead of focusing solely on calling out her sin and holding her accountable, I focused on being gentle and loving toward her. Something changed during that lunch. Through my gentleness, she saw God's true grace.

From then on, she worked harder on her problem. She didn't work harder because she desired to change more than she did before. She had long wanted to change her ways. She worked harder because the gentleness of the Holy Spirit reminded her that God's love wasn't going away. God's grace was here to stay, and that impacted her more and held her more accountable than I ever could.

5. Patient

Patience. Ahh—one of the most difficult things to live out every day. When you are frustrated, remind yourself:

- *You do not have a helicopter view of everyone's lives.* You're simply seeing their stories and choices from one angle. Jesus has an all-seeing view of everyone you meet. He knows about their hard days. He knows about their mistakes. He knows their childhood baggage that causes them to hurt you. Maybe we should listen to Him to know how to treat others. Your friend may say you should "tell off" those who hurt you. But Jesus, the One who knows all things and all people, says to "love your enemies and pray for those who persecute you" (Matthew 5:44).
- *You are to watch and listen for God's timing, not your own.* What a shame it would be if we missed out on our purpose because we were in a rush. Be patient with yourself when you mess up at work. Be patient with the family members who keep bringing you down. Love others and everyone well, no matter where they are. No rush is needed to get things right.
- *You are called to your "right now."* Being in your "right now" is more important than being right. We want to hustle in our careers and climb the ladder of success. We want to do things "right." Our society has told us we should get the promotions, constantly move up in our careers, get married at a certain age, and live life the "right" way. We crave living our lives "right"

because we think purpose is something you have to work for. We think purpose is a one-size-fits-all package, and if it doesn't look like Ashley's timeline, we are living life "wrong" and are late. That is a lie. Purpose happens in your everyday life. Your purpose is unique to you. Be patient with yourself if you don't feel like you have the career, influence, or position to do big things. When you live for your big Savior, you are doing big things. And this, my friend, happens in your everyday life. Kingdom things equal big things. Be patient with yourself so you can be purposeful.

6. Childlike

In Matthew 19:14, Jesus said, "Let the little children come to me, and do not hinder them, for the kingdom of heaven belongs to such as these."

Children are honest and obedient if they know who to follow. Children believe and trust without needing proof. As we grow older, we start to become realistic instead of holistic. We stop believing in miracles and abandon our childhood dreams.

I want to dream big dreams. I want to believe in the impossible and chase adventure. I care about living a life that sees the big God we serve. If I want to see God do big things, then I have to let go of my habit of being realistic. If I want to stop being realistic, I have to be like a child and stop worrying about being right.

7. Eagerly optimistic

"So, you really think you can write a book?"

A cute fraternity boy said this to me once when I told him I wanted to write a book and publish it traditionally. He laughed as he said it. After that encounter, I was reluctant to tell my peers I was trying to publish a book. I was so scared about how stupid I would look if it didn't work out. Would people think I was a loser?

Life is too short to care about what "makes sense." Did it make sense that a nineteen-year-old could write a book? No. But I was optimistic. And I wasn't just optimistic; I was eager. I was happily chasing the impossible. This was all out of character for me, and the more I reflect on that college girl e-mailing what felt like 104 literary agents, the more I am reminded that the Holy Spirit will give you the push and energy you need.

And you know, even if I had never become an author, I would feel good about listening to the Spirit and not what some frat boy thought was right.

8. Alert

I want to be ready for God to use me for big things. I can't expect to do big things unless I notice my big Savior. It's important to be alert every day. If you waste precious moments trying to prove to others that you are right, you'll miss out on the opportunity to see Jesus. And if you aren't alert and noticing your Savior, you'll never be able to live out your purpose.

I pray that you do not yell at managers because it is a Tuesday, you're annoyed, and you are sure you are right. I pray that you and I can work on living lives that are more kind than self-righteous.

When we follow Jesus, we have nothing to prove. We serve a Savior, not a scorecard. Let go of your desire to be right, and hold on to your sweet Savior.

Real Talk

- How did the good Samaritan in Jesus' story love his neighbor well? What did the priest and Levite do differently?

- In what situations in your life can you focus on being kind more than right?
- This chapter describes eight characteristics that we can display instead of trying to prove we are right. Which characteristic stuck out to you the most, and why?

19

WHEN OUR STRUGGLES ARE SECRET

About two years after my first book released, I was traveling and telling girls how loved they are. I was offering them all the right answers. But insecurity had crept back into my own thoughts.

This is the chapter of this book that I did not want to write. I can't help but wonder what my church will think when I make this admission. I can't help but wonder how my grandmother will feel when she reads this. I can't help but wonder how the girls who see me as a role model will feel. I can't help but wonder what you will think as you read this chapter.

Isn't it ironic? I can write books about God's love and living in truth, yet I still find myself holding on to shame. If I can sit here and struggle with being honest, I can't help but wonder how you feel on the other side of this book. I can't help but wonder what you are holding on to. I can't help but wonder what pressure you feel to hide your weaknesses.

So I wrote this chapter anyway because I know trusting in God means letting go of our shame. Let me tell you about my secret struggle.

I messed up one night. I ate Mexican food with a friend, came home, and cried because of how much I had eaten. I had gained weight recently and was frustrated that I had eaten so much. Then I stood over the toilet and remembered a way to get rid of the food I had consumed. I knew a way to make up for my mistake.

And I did it.

That night, I returned to a secret habit. I woke up the next morning and gave a sermon for the students at my church. One of the girls came up to talk with me afterward, and I started crying. I blamed my allergies when, in reality, I was crying because I didn't understand how I could be a role model for girls while I was still struggling with an old habit.

At that point I had not gone to counseling because of my pride. I was independent. I thought I could handle anything. So when I received an e-mail from work that offered free counseling for director-level positions, I dismissed it at first. My church had a counseling center, and I did not trust anyone at church with my secrets. I was supposed to be everyone's role model, and I couldn't be the one who was messed up. Then I continued reading the e-mail and noted that counseling would be with an outside group of counselors and confidential.

I could go to a confidential session, I thought.

I was in a season when I couldn't trust anyone, and the idea of having someone contractually obligated to not spill my dirt sounded healthy. I had never wanted to be that girl who needed counseling, but the truth was, I was exhausted from struggling with my insecurity.

I visited the counselor. I went again. I finally told two friends about my secret struggle so I could allow myself to stop denying it. I began to take steps the counselor suggested.

Now I see the importance of counseling. The reason I had struggled to understand counseling for many years was that I was prideful. But I knew deep down I needed a Christian counselor. I highly recommend counseling and am an advocate for it now. I realize our problems in this world will never be cured. Sin is still here. But with the help that comes from letting others in, we can point ourselves to Jesus, even on the hard days.

I also see the importance of licensed psychiatrists who prescribe medicine, doctors, dietitians, and residential programs. There are many options for healing, and each person has their own unique needs to begin this process. If you struggle with anything pertaining to mental health, please tell someone and seek spiritual health and also professional programs. Doctors have gifts given by God to provide the care you need.

I also realized through this process that following Jesus isn't a guarantee of happily ever after. Following Jesus is a choice you make every day. When you accept Christ in your heart, you make a choice. A beautiful choice. But every day when you wake up, you have to decide to follow God that day. There is no one-stop shopping cure for insecurity. And in a world that consistently tempts you to steer away from God's truth, you have to choose God every moment.

If truth sets us free, then know the truth. Know Scripture. Fight your battle with His words. Jesus said, "If you hold to my teaching, you are really my disciples. Then you will know the truth, and the truth will set you free" (John 8:31–32). Shame and pretending you have it all together won't allow the truth to set you free.

The Next Time You Are Tempted . . .

The next time you and I fight an old battle again, the next time we get tempted to fall back into our old ways and secret struggles, let's do these four things.

1. Decide you want to fight. ———————————

Put on the armor of God, described in Ephesians 6:10–18. Go into spiritual battle. It's easy to see our struggle but do nothing about it. We think, *That's just the way it is.* We get tired of fighting and give up. Stop giving up. In John 16:33, Jesus said, "I have told you these things, so that in me you may have peace. In this world you will have trouble. But take heart! I have overcome the world."

Yes, living in this world is difficult, and we all face doubt and insecurity. But Jesus has overcome the world. When we choose Him daily, we have Someone on our side who will fight when we are weak. Let's not allow our struggles to win!

2. Talk with the One who holds truth. ———————

Stop believing lies. Stop turning to the world for comfort and answers that it can't provide. Open your Bible. Open your prayer journal. If you don't have a prayer journal, create or buy one. If we don't get to know Jesus through prayer and reading His Word, we will forget to choose Him. Know Him. Know His Word. He is truth, and when we talk to Him, we receive the truth. Truth can only set us free if we know who holds the truth.

3. Seek healing instead of trying to prove yourself. ——

I often forget that I have nothing to prove, just a Savior to love. Jesus is not looking for perfection; He just wants me. He wants the honest me. The me hiding in the bathroom tempted to punish myself. The me who wanted to hide my fears behind a locked bathroom door. But Jesus wants an honest me. The real me. *Just me.*

He wants me to run to Him and choose Him.

When we live our lives trying to prove something to others and even Jesus, we aren't living out of truth. When we try to prove something, we live out of pride, and that is a sin.

I had to let go of my wrong impression of counseling and finally seek healing. I didn't have to prove to anyone that I had it all together. The first step to my healing was understanding that I have a Savior who says, "Come as you are," not one who says, "Fix yourself first."

4. Put trust into action.

We have to act out of trust in our lives. Trust that our battle is not too hard for God. Trust that obedience won't make our lives less fun. Trust that God is good at being God and that we should choose Him. Jesus went to the cross for us. The least we can do is trust that He is good and that He is on our side.

When you face a battle, do yourself a favor: be honest. Be honest with others; be honest with yourself. Take a step closer to healing, and take a step closer to the truth. Your Savior loves and cares for you. Now, live out that trust.

Real Talk

- What is the chapter of your story that you would hate to write? Why?
- How have you put trust into action lately?
- What does it mean to put on the armor of God? Read Ephesians 6:10–18 for a description of this spiritual armor.
- What is one way this week that you can remind yourself of God's truth?

20

WHEN CHRISTIANS SAY ANNOYING THINGS

"The Devil uses yoga pants to distract men. I don't get how 'Christian' women can wear yoga pants."

I'll never forget that statement from a fellow camp staffer. I'll never forget because as she said that, I was laying out my outfit for the next day, which included my temptation-trapping, attention-seeking, Devil-used yoga pants.

Oops.

I didn't know my pants held that much power compared to the whole gospel! The Devil was out here using my stretchy, comfy pants to distract men from knowing Jesus. If they wound up going to hell, it must be because on one cold Thursday morning I decided to wear yoga pants to the grocery store. My pants could lead people to *hell*! Who knew my pants and my tushy held so much power?

I laughed about the comment to a friend. I know my fellow staffer had a good heart, but I also would have loved to throw her into my public high school in south Louisiana for one day. This girl was more sheltered than me and most of my friends.

After laughing with my friend, I told her, "I'm sick and tired of annoying things Christians say."

I have a journal page dedicated to annoying things Christians say. The yoga pants comment made the list. But I've noticed that many other annoying things Christians say have come from my own lips.

In high school I remember tweeting about how some girls wore little to no clothes. I'm embarrassed to admit that I judged girls who wore immodest clothes and was not afraid to tell everyone how I felt. I even defended my tweet as standing up for my faith. As if the whole gospel was dependent on my telling girls their dresses were too short.

I called the tweet standing up for my faith. God called it being prideful.

Then after school, I moved to Waco, Texas, for university. The Bible Belt, small-city Texas life was far from the culture of the New Orleans suburbs where I grew up. Clothes were more conservative in my college town. Suddenly, I went from being the prude, innocent girl to the partying, wild girl. From being the one judging to the one being judged. God knew I needed humility, and I also needed to taste how sweet His grace really is.

As a student at Baylor University, I received a text from a girl I barely knew telling me that my shorts were too short. I invited her to get frozen yogurt together so we could talk. She had made assumptions about my family life, my walk with God, and the mistakes I was making—all from one outfit! I looked her in the eyes and will never forget how surprised she seemed when I said, "Hey, do you know I am a virgin? Because I think you're assuming I am not."

My virginity didn't matter to the conversation, but her assumptions about my walk and sins were all wrong. She thought my shorts told a story of a girl who hooked up all the time. She assumed she knew my story. Yet she had never asked for my story. My story actually was one of pain, but she couldn't know that without asking.

I left our meeting feeling unknown, hurt, and unseen. She had judged my whole faith based on one pair of shorts. In that season, I was dealing with insecurity, loneliness, and pain. I needed her to see my heart, not my shorts.

Don't Be a Stumbling Block

Christians can be annoying. Christians can be judgmental. Christians can make assumptions about others based off of worldly labels. Maybe, like me, you're tired of this too. If this frustrates you, find hope in the fact that the gospel is bigger than the issues of this world.

I love the message found in Romans 14:1–13. I recommend you read the whole passage, but I'll be highlighting some important points based off verses in this passage. For context, know that Paul wrote Romans as a letter to the Christians residing in the area. Rome was very ethnically diverse during this time. Paul used this passage to encourage the Christians in Rome to stop debating over matters that are disputable. He encouraged them to allow Jesus to be the judge.

1. "Accept the one whose faith is weak, without quarreling over disputable matters" (v. 1).

So often the church notices details instead of the heart. When we focus too much on addressing details over heart issues, we fail to see the need for the gospel. When I look at the way Jesus lived, I see Someone who cared first about making others feel loved. This doesn't mean He agreed with everyone's lifestyle choices, and this doesn't mean He didn't call others away from sin. It just means His first encounter was one with open arms rather than pointed fingers.

How do you first encounter someone who is struggling? Are you living with a posture of open arms? Or are you living with a posture of pointed fingers? The gospel is too important to position yourself wrongly. Again, so often we focus more on being right than kind. I want to live out the truth, but I also want to live out love. Jesus is love *and* truth.

2. "If we live, we live for the Lord; and if we die, we die for the Lord. So, whether we live or die, we belong to the Lord" (v. 8).

It is easy to speak our minds, which hold what we believe is right and true. But I would rather speak the Spirit than my mind. The Spirit is one of "love, joy, peace, forbearance, kindness, goodness, faithfulness, gentleness and self-control" (Galatians 5:22–23). The Spirit knows how to control my tongue. The Spirit makes it possible for me to see others with love as my lens.

Our lives are not our own, so our assumptions about others should not be our own either. Be the one who cares more about showing love than being heard. Be the one who cares more about speaking the Spirit than your mind. Be the one who lives for the Lord and not the one who lives to be right.

3. "So then, each of us will give an account of ourselves to God. Therefore let us stop passing judgment on one another. Instead, make up your mind not to put any stumbling block or obstacle in the way of a brother or sister" (vv. 12–13).

I think we have depersonalized the gospel. Don't get me wrong—some truth is universal. We are all made in the image of God. Jesus was born from a virgin. Jesus was God's Son. Jesus died on the cross for our sins, was buried, and rose from the dead three days later. Because of these unchanging truths, we have an opportunity to live with Him while in this world and for eternity.

However, our faith is our own. God manages to talk to each of us uniquely. Each of us will face our Maker in the end and give an account of our lives. Each of us has Him in our lives now, wanting to join us in an everyday relationship.

I will not be giving an account to God about Jessica's outfit choice at the music festival. I bet God will ask me if I loved her, though. I will not be asked to explain why Chad cheated on his girlfriend. I bet God will want to know whether I showed grace to Sam or talked poorly about him at brunch with the girls.

Iron does sharpen iron (Proverbs 27:17). Once you invite others to friendship and they have seen you love them, then you should be able to call them up. You should push them to turn away from their sin. Calling someone up, though, is not calling someone out. A sign on the side of the street doesn't help with the heart issue someone is facing. But breakfast and a hug will show that you love and want more for them.

When you judge others out of your own pride, you become a stumbling block. Others will never be able to see the love of God if all they hear is your opinion. When you allow your opinion to be louder than God's grace, your pride wins, not Jesus. When you live out of pride, you are saying your opinion is greater than the love of God.

Let the Spirit Work

Don't be the reason someone forgets who they are. The Holy Spirit will convict them of their sin. When you speak from the Spirit, truth will be gentle and stir their heart to change. But if you speak your mind, only your pride will be heard.

So whether you're the one who has said hurtful things or you're the one who has been hurt and judged by Christians, let's drop the pride. *To the hurt and judged*: stop allowing the judgment of others to be

louder than the love of God. God calls you up, not out. You are called
to please Him, not other Christians.

To the one who has judged: there's grace for you too. Start today
with a posture of open arms instead of pointed fingers. You can
live a life of love if you're willing to speak from the Spirit instead of
your mind.

Real Talk

- What is the difference between calling someone up and
  calling someone out?
- Has someone displayed to you a posture of open arms
  after you messed up? If so, what did they say and do?
  How did that make you feel?
- How do we speak from the Spirit instead of from our
  minds?
- Have you judged someone? If so, what happened?
- Have you been judged by someone? If so, how did you
  feel about yourself?

Part 5

AM I THE ONLY ONE CONFUSED ABOUT HOW TO BE AN ADULT?

21

WHEN WE DON'T KNOW WHAT WE "SHOULD" BE DOING

I was a junior in high school when I had my first kiss. In my high school, that made me a late bloomer. I was judged by peers for not dating. I was called "weird," "prude," and other names I try to forget.

Before I had my first kiss, I remember feeling pathetic: *I should have had my first kiss by now!*

Isn't it funny how everyone else always has an opinion about what we should be doing? That is not just a high school problem—it's a life problem.

An older woman recently told me this at church: "I just think right now, you should really be looking for a husband. You don't want to get to twenty-five and not have a husband."

I know she meant well. I know she did not mean to hurt my feelings. But guess what? *She did!* She not only hurt my feelings but also

147

made me think I was doing something wrong. My life was not falling into place the way she thought it should be. And because of that, she thought I was a failure.

Should We Be Doing That?

We have all been there. I remember thinking in high school that I should be dating more guys because I needed more experience when it came to dating.

Then I hit my twenties.

Your twenties are weird because no matter what you're doing, you always feel like you are doing something wrong. There are a million contradicting statements of what you "should" be doing. I think every season is like that, though. You can't help but look to your left and to your right and think, *Should I be doing that?*

Some of your friends have graduated college. Some of your friends are on a fifth year. Some dropped out of college after their first semester. Some never went to college at all.

Some of your friends are married. Some are engaged. Some are happy being single. And some are still spending their Friday nights on the dance floor.

Some of your friends have their dream jobs. Some are just trying to get by.

Some of your friends have kids, and some still act like kids.

Welcome to life in your twenties.

Your "adult years" have begun, yet you're still confused about your identity. You're old enough to know better but young enough to think you can run away from the future.

It's easy to spend your life looking at your friends and peers and thinking:

I should be doing that.

I should know what I want to be when I grow up.

I should be dating.

I should be married.

I should be single.

I should have graduated by now.

I should have a cleaner past.

I should have a messier past.

I should have kids.

I shouldn't have kids.

I should have my dream job.

I should have enough money to go on at least one nice vacation.

But the beautiful thing about your life is that there are no "shoulds." You have freedom and free will. You don't have to be in school studying a major you hate. You don't have to be married or have kids. There are no rules. And despite what others tell you, there is not one path everyone should follow.

Stop comparing your life to someone else's. Stop exhausting yourself with everyone else's shoulds.

You are not her. You are not your friend, your peer, or that girl you stalk on Instagram.

You are you. And the main thing you "should" be doing in your life is falling in love with your Creator and pursuing who He created you to be.

Your Greatest Calling

The world tells you that your purpose is to chase success, a hefty bank account, and a decent social life. But your purpose comes from your Creator. Your greatest calling is to live for your Creator and to appreciate who He created—a wonderful human being who has some flaws and great purpose.

The most beautiful thing about your life is that you have the opportunity to fall in love with your path. Your handcrafted path was given to you by your Creator.

Your path might not look like others', but your path is exclusively yours. And God is leading you where you were meant to be all along.

To my fellow overthinkers, relax. Breathe in; breathe out. Look at where your feet are planted. God brought you this far for a reason. You are doing okay. You will be okay.

Wake up each day and become eager to give your life to the One who breathed life into you. That is all you should be doing. You don't have to chase perfection and the world's standards for your twenties. Simply chase Jesus, striving to talk to Him and live for Him.

Close the dating app. Take a nap. Go to work. And look up. God placed every star right where it needs to be. Why don't you trust the One who hung the stars and painted the sea to place your life together? He knows what you should be doing. He knows where you are and where you will be. Let go of the independence you craved when you were younger, and fall back into dependence on Him. You need Him. You should love and trust Him. And that's the only "should" you should be doing.

If you know who holds your past, present, and future, you will not be panicked about your timetable. You won't be overly influenced by what others think your timeline should be. Live for Jesus in your today, and trust Him with your tomorrow. And please remember that your life is different from everyone else's because you are different from everyone else. That is worthy of celebration!

Trust God's Plan

Proverbs 3:5–6 says, "Trust in the LORD with all your heart and lean not on your own understanding; in all your ways submit to him, and he will make your paths straight."

Friend, my prayer is that you and I can trust God with His plan. Our limited understanding does not make sense. It can't. If we lean into what makes sense to us and the expectations everyone else has for us, our paths will never be straight. We'll worry. We'll experience disappointment. But if we trust in the Lord and lean on His perfect understanding, we will experience joy in the unknown. If we obey His wishes and trust His will for our lives, He will make our paths straight. Straight doesn't mean easy; it means the path is taking us where we need to go and giving us the opportunity to sense God in our lives.

If the lady from my church is reading this chapter and still worried about my dating life, I hope she realizes that I have God on my side. I am not trusting in her understanding for my life. I don't mean that rudely because I'm not even relying on *my* understanding for my life. I am tired of living a life that reflects what others want. I am leaning on God and trusting His understanding of my life.

God's timing is always perfect. Stop questioning. Trust Him. What a shame it would be if we missed out on our purpose because we were too busy worrying about what others thought we should be doing.

If you are trusting in God and leaning on His understanding, then you are exactly where you are supposed to be. Trust that. Believe that.

Real Talk

- What is a "should" you often hear from others in your life?
- Have you ever become exhausted by trying to live for others? Why was that so exhausting?
- How can you trust that God's timing is the right timing?
- Write a prayer about trusting God to be God. Ask Him to reveal the importance of embracing where you are today.

22

WHEN WE HAVE SOMETHING TO PROVE

Fun fact: if you had googled my name in early 2020, you would have come across a website that reported my net worth as $14 million.

This fact is actually more "funny" than "fun" because the report was far from the truth. I actually had overdrawn on my bank account the week before. At Taco Bell.

I did not learn of my supposed net worth by googling myself. Instead, I found out after several guy friends from high school suddenly started hitting me up. One guy in particular, whom I had known since middle school, contacted me. I freaked out a little. I felt like an insecure seventh grader who just received a dash of attention from the star player of the football team.

I FaceTimed one of the only friends I still talk to from high school to tell her that I'd heard from this guy out of the blue because, yes, I'm that pathetic. My friend laughed and told me, "Grace, did you know some people have been sending this link around from a website saying your net worth is $14 million? That is probably why he reached out."

I laughed hard and looked up the website. There it was: my name, next to $14 million. So the cute boy from seventh grade thought I was worth $14 million. Even better, all the people from high school who rejected me, hurt me, and even made fun of me back then were now reaching out to me because they thought I was rolling in the dough.

Is it bad that that was kind of fun for me? It felt like sweet revenge. Except I wasn't rich. I was struggling to pay rent!

The sad part of the story was that when I started hearing from my old friends, I felt like I had finally proved myself to all my peers. I was a grown woman, yet I was happy that the hot seventh-grade boy and mean girl from middle school thought I was successful. Why did I still care so much about their opinions? Why did I search for validation through what they thought of me? Why did people miles away from me still hold an importance when it came to my sense of worth?

Why did I still feel like I had something to prove?

We have all been this way at least once. We feel the need to prove ourselves. Maybe you want to prove to your ex that you have moved on, to your parents that you are doing well for yourself, or to your old peers that you are successful. Maybe you strive to prove to your followers that you are pretty, to your friends that you deserve an invite, or to your coworkers that you're a hard worker.

Living as though you have something to prove is tiring. You might see a random article that says you are worth $14 million and feel good for a second. You might feel like you proved something. But you'll wake up the next day and feel like you have more to prove.

It's exhausting. It's never-ending.

What Happens When We Have
Something to Prove?

When you and I keep living like we have something to prove, we deflect three important things.

1. We deflect truth.

When we live for other people's approval, we deflect our true selves. We try to fit other people's molds and avoid becoming who God created us to be. What a shame it would be if we exhausted ourselves living a life that was only a lie.

2. We deflect Jesus.

When we are trying to prove ourselves, we are essentially saying that the cross was not enough. We are saying the person Jesus died for was not enough. Instead of picking up our crosses to follow Him, we are picking up others' opinions and following them. Let's live for Jesus and stop living like we have something to prove to the world. The cross was enough. It's time to stop deflecting the One who loves us as we are.

3. We deflect grace.

I used to believe that "success is the best revenge." I thought proving myself in this world would show my ex that he made a mistake, the mean girl that she should have been nice to me, and that one family member who doubts me would see that they are wrong.

When you and I spend our time trying to be successful to prove others wrong, we don't have time to give them grace. We cannot live out love and also live like we have something to prove. We cannot give grace while also trying to seek revenge.

Deflection is a defense mechanism we use to protect ourselves from reflecting on the truth and our true feelings. The world teaches us to deflect our emotions and truth to protect ourselves. We deflect truth by creating an exterior that says we are "realistic." We deflect our emotions by creating an exterior that says, "I don't care." We deflect our purpose by creating an exterior of being busy. We are exhausted because we spend our energy deflecting instead of reflecting on our emotions and Jesus' love. When we reflect on our feelings and focus our attention to Jesus' love, we reflect a life that trusts.

Learn to Reflect Instead of Deflect

What does reflection actually look like? Here are two things you and I can do to reflect instead of deflect.

1. Write down our true feelings.

Often when I know what I am feeling is a sin or not right, I deflect it. I give the "Christian" response. But just because we know the correct answer does not mean we believe it to be true. We can say, "God has a plan" but still not trust that He has a good plan. If we don't admit our sin, we can't receive God's grace. If we don't admit that we struggle, we can't receive God's salvation. So let's not allow the fear of being wrong to stop us from growing. Grab your journal and write down how you truly feel.

2. Fight sin with truth.

After you write down your true feelings, write down truth. Write truth that comes from Scripture, those who love you, and anything God tells you.

When you and I are tempted by sin or tempted to deny His goodness, we must fight our battles with His truth. His truth is armor and a weapon, used both for protection and to fight away the Enemy.

The Truth Will Set You Free

Jesus gave us an example of how to use God's Word as a weapon to defend against attacks from our enemy, Satan.

> Jesus was led by the Spirit into the wilderness to be tempted by the devil. After fasting forty days and forty nights, he was hungry. The tempter came to him and said, "If you are the Son of God, tell these stones to become bread."
>
> Jesus answered, "It is written: 'Man shall not live on bread alone, but on every word that comes from the mouth of God.'"
>
> Then the devil took him to the holy city and had him stand on the highest point of the temple. "If you are the Son of God," he said, "throw yourself down. For it is written:
>
> "'He will command his angels concerning you,
>   and they will lift you up in their hands,
>   so that you will not strike your foot against a stone.'"
>
> Jesus answered him, "It is also written: 'Do not put the Lord your God to the test.'"
>
> Again, the devil took him to a very high mountain and showed him all the kingdoms of the world and their splendor. "All this I will give you," he said, "if you bow down and worship me."
>
> Jesus said to him, "Away from me, Satan! For it is written: 'Worship the Lord your God, and serve him only.'"
>
> Then the devil left him, and angels came and attended him. (Matthew 4:1–11)

Jesus was approached by Satan. He was tempted. Satan made sense. Satan was realistic. Satan was trying to manipulate Jesus into believing that his words were true. But Jesus knew Scripture. If you want the truth to "set you free" (John 8:32), then you'd better be like Jesus and know the truth and use it to fight your battles.

Yes, reflect on your thoughts, but also reflect on Scripture. Open your Bible. Pray. You need to know the truth in order to be set free. Freedom is given to everyone, but wisdom is gained through Him and His Word. When you are wise, it's easier for you to notice your freedom and fight your battles.

We have made reading our Bibles more difficult than it needs to be. I remember being a "veteran" Christian who picked up her Bible only on Sundays. I remember highlighting words to make it look as if I read my Bible more than I did. (How pathetic!)

I think many of us have been in that situation. We are scared to start reading Scripture because we don't know where to begin. Or maybe we're scared we won't understand what we read.

Reading the Bible does not start with a certain tool or a specific chapter. It starts simply when you start. When you open your Bible and decide you are ready to know the truth. When you have exhausted yourself over and over again with Christian sayings that aren't Scripture. When your doubts make your faith feel weak. All of those are products of not knowing the truth.

I have a feeling that you, too, might be exhausted from proving yourself to people and not trusting Jesus. If that is you, get to know the truth. If you're tired of chasing everyone's approval, open your Bible and start chasing God's truth.

Real Talk

- Does reading the Bible intimidate you? Why or why not?
- Find a friend to be your accountability partner. Text her after you finish reading your Bible each day. Create

goals together about how you will challenge yourself to read God's Word.

- Do you struggle with caring about what people think of you? How do you think Jesus responds to this battle you face?
- When Jesus was tempted, He knew Scripture and was able to use it to protect Himself from Satan's attacks. Search for other Bible passages or verses that remind you His Word is true and our source of hope. Write down those additional passages so that on difficult days, you can reflect on His Word.

23

WHEN LIFE SUDDENLY CHANGES

I bought my house when I was twenty-three. It's small, but cute. I live right next to some of my best friends, who are three middle-aged women. They are cooler than me. They dress better than me. They love better than me. They make me so thankful.

Shout out to Kathy, Adair, and Candace! You have made Orlando home for me. I call them my "mom friends."

I was happy and proud of myself for buying a house at my age. So happy, in fact, that I posted about my new house on Instagram 100 percent to brag. I mean, why else do people post their accomplishments on social media? To brag to the public and their grandmother! Right?

I did that!

Girl boss!

Proving everyone wrong!

Success!

But then the coronavirus hit, and everything changed. *Of course I'm the girl who buys a house right before the stock market crashes. That is so me. Unlucky.* But I still had a salaried job. I might be the girl who had bad luck about when to purchase a home, but I would never be that girl without a job. I hustled hard. I worked hard. I brought value to my ministry job at a megachurch that surely had an emergency budget for moments like this.

Wrong.

Most of my friends were working from home, but I was still working in the office, quickly creating an eight-week social media plan and storing graphics I made to Google Drive. I was told that everyone would be working from home on Thursday.

On Thursday, while working from home, I received a mass e-mail from a pastor I love and respect saying there would be a phone meeting at 10:00 a.m. I continued making graphics and offering to help other staff members however I could.

At 10:00 a.m., I got a call saying they needed to do budget cuts. They told me that I would be temporarily laid off starting at noon that day. Later, I heard through the grapevine that the layoffs weren't temporary. As I write this, I have no clue if I will ever work at my amazing, life-giving ministry job again.

The call ended with an automated "good-bye" from the hosting system. It sounded as if Alexa had said good-bye to me. A robotic good-bye.

Good-bye to two years of community and relationships formed at the church.

Good-bye to my students in the student ministry for which I served as girls minister.

Good-bye to all my hard work to develop a digital plan for our ministry.

Good-bye.

I felt like Taylor Swift when Joe Jonas broke up with her over a phone call. My favorite artist and the queen of breakup anthems was broken up with by her serious superstar boyfriend Joe Jonas on a less-than-one-minute phone call. Granted, now I see that a phone call was the safest and best way to do this layoff during the health crisis. I also understand the church's need to protect their budget during unforeseen times. They made the decision they had to in order to protect the church, and I do respect that. It's just that now was in a pickle.

I sat in my new, empty house, with barely any furniture, and cried. I had spent two wonderful years in ministry at a place that broke up with me quickly and impersonally, in my opinion.

I was mad. I was hurt. I was in trouble financially. I had budgeted for my mortgage expecting to receive paychecks. My dad had told me, "Grace, anything can happen. Are you sure you want to buy this house?"

I said yes. I insisted I would be fine.

Father knows best. *Sorry, Dad. I didn't foresee a global pandemic in the near future.*

I felt all the feelings.

I drafted texts I didn't send.

I practiced conversations that never happened.

I listened to breakup songs and related to them more than ever.

I wondered how I would be able to move on from this setback. I had many unanswered questions and feelings during this process. But most importantly, I felt sadness, like I lost something close to my heart. I wanted to be the girl boss who bought the house and excelled at life but felt like no matter what I did, I ended up short.

Finally, a close mentor told me, "You know what the feminist thing would be to do? Outearn them. Change lives without this career you were let go from. Thank them for what you learned and move on to where God is calling you. Spread the gospel, and use your gifts for Jesus' name. Don't let them slow you down; let them speed you up."

I don't think I'll ever have the answers I desire or the conclusion I crave. I may never understand why God even allowed the coronavirus to happen when it killed so many people and caused so many others to be left in a similar situation as me, or worse. But harboring resentment and frustration was not going to make me feel better, and it surely was not going to spread the gospel.

Granted, outearning men is not something I want to strive for, nor is it something I want others to strive for. I do believe women should push for equal pay. But taking rejection and turning it into something that pushes you to something greater—yeah, I want to be a part of that.

The best girl-boss tip I have for you is to know your foundation, build your life on something great, and move on. Wave and smile. God closes doors to lead you to where you are meant to be.

Let me be honest with you, though: we as women still face discrimination. My friends of color still face discrimination. Where there is discrimination, I hope you fight. However, I hope during the fight that you remember God is with you and leading you. God is leading you to Him. Trust that God is building a better tomorrow for someone else, fight for what is right, and move on to your next step with the confidence that you have played your part. Tomorrow will be better because you fought in the Lord's name.

I realized through this heartbreak that I was building my life's foundation and security on my smart financial decisions. My wealth and comfort from having a stable job and a published book made me feel great. But God didn't call us to build our house on the American economy, great relationships with superiors, or even our own comfort.

During my season of being laid off, I wrestled with insecurity, doubt, and pain. I also gained a new perspective. See, in our mountaintop experiences, we can see our lives more clearly. We can see that the valleys led us to the mountaintops, the hike was worth it, and the sun has always been close by. But when you're in your valleys, you have to have trust and hope.

Trust and hope become the rope that helps guide you when you can't see where you are going. You have no clue at the time if the view will be worth it. But you grab the rope anyway, hold tight, and take it step by step. You have to trust that God is good and remember that this world and our pain are temporary. You need to hope that you'll see the mountain again. You have to put one foot in front of the other and press on to your purpose.

You may never understand why. I don't care how confrontational you are—you might never get the answers you want for why things happened. But what you can control is your next move.

Build Your Life on Jesus

On my difficult days in that season, I reflected on this passage:

> Everyone who hears these words of mine and puts them into prac-
> tice is like a wise man who built his house on the rock. The rain
> came down, the streams rose, and the winds blew and beat against
> that house; yet it did not fall, because it had its foundation on the
> rock. But everyone who hears these words of mine and does not
> put them into practice is like a foolish man who built his house
> on sand. The rain came down, the streams rose, and the winds
> blew and beat against that house, and it fell with a great crash.
> (Matthew 7:24–27)

This passage provided me peace because it did not say I would never deal with storms. It did not promise me sunshine and a Hallmark-movie life. In fact, this passage says the rain came down, the streams rose, and the wind beat against the house.

In this world, you'll experience frustration and hurt. You will have breakups and layoffs. Those can remind us that our foundation is in our control. The storm is out of our control. But what and who we build our life on is in our control.

I want to be clear that I love and respect my church that laid me off. I love and respect the pastors in leadership and trust they are in their positions for a reason. Through this season of heartache, I learned how much I valued my independence versus how much I depended on God. That was the issue. My pride separated me from true dependence. The layoff was never the problem—I was. Layoffs will happen, jobs will be lost, people will communicate in the wrong way. But God is in control, and I needed to give Him my trust.

Building your life on Jesus means that when the economy tanks, you realize He is still in control. Building your life on Jesus means that when life doesn't go how you planned, you trust in His name. Building your life on Jesus means that even in the unknown and in the storm, you safely enjoy the comfort and peace that come from knowing that the purpose of life is about something greater than what you're upset about now.

What to Do During Your Next Storm

During your next storm, try these six things:

1. *Feel all the feels.* Nothing frustrates me more than people who say, "It could be worse" while someone is mourning their situation. It is not a sin to be upset. Just because someone else's whole body hurts does not mean that your arm does not hurt. Your emotions are your emotions. They are valid.

2. *Find peace in the One who is more powerful than the storm.* You are not promised sunshine, but you are given Him. Life

is a mystery. Stop praying for answers and start praying for understanding. Understanding does not come from answers; it comes from true trust.

3. *Check your foundation.* God doesn't tell you when the storm is coming, but He tells you to be prepared. Make sure your worth and value are founded in Him. If your pain is breaking you, you probably aren't built on the ultimate Healer. Your pain can sting, and your pain can suck. But your pain does not have the power to destroy you if your life is ultimately built on Him. If you do feel like your world is falling apart, check what your world is built on.

4. *Remember that you were a child of God before you were a girl boss.* I get it. We want to feel empowered and feel like we are in control. But it's exhausting to be a girl boss if you don't see that you are supposed to first be a child of God. Buy a house, start a business, find independence post-breakup, and you do you, girl. I hope and pray that you succeed and do big things. I hope you get degrees or work doing what you love. I hope you find joy in whatever you do daily. But before you can be a boss, you have to know who you are following. You can't lead without being led. You can't succeed if you don't realize Jesus already won. Life is never about what you do; it is about what Jesus has done. Do big things, celebrate your success, but celebrate Jesus more. He is the reason you have the ability to try things on this earth. And He is the reason this earth is nothing compared to eternity with Him. Finding my worth in my ability to buy a house was like building my foundation on sand. Finding your worth in your success, looks, relationships, or even family is like building your life on sand. Know that your worth comes from Him.

5. *Become dependent on God.* I know it's easy to crave independence. In our society, independence is a sign of success. But I hope you have moments when only Jesus can make a way

forward. I hope the storm rocks you and reminds you to hold tight to Him. Become dependent on who He is, and you will genuinely see His power. Being independent is great, but never allow your independence to make you think, *I've got this.* You don't—God's got this. Know His power, or watch yourself fall at the first storm.

6. *Know that you are going to be okay.* Right now, you might be experiencing exhaustion from dealing with a storm. But the storm is temporary. Sometimes everything has to fall apart so you can start to rebuild. The neighborhood I live in is known for having investors buy old houses, tear them down, and build something new from the ground up. Immediately, their value is more than triple the purchase price. If everything in your life is falling apart, maybe God is saying, *Let's try this again—My way.* Don't shake your fist and ask God, "Why?" Instead, go to your knees, pray, and try to rebuild following His way.

I hope you are prepared when storms come. People will hurt you, and winds will blow. Life isn't about what happens around you; it is about what happens in your heart. I pray that you find energy in knowing that with every storm comes an opportunity—an opportunity to test your foundation.

Your worth and strength come from God. I get so tired of hearing people say their strength comes from "within." During my layoff and struggle financially and emotionally, I realized I had no more strength left within. If I wanted to get through my crappy days, I had to find my strength from Him. I had to rebuild my life and remind myself that He is boss, not me.

Real Talk

- Have you faced rejection from someone you admire? If so, when?
- God never said that there won't be storms. In fact, He advised to be prepared for storms. How can you make God your foundation now so you are prepared for the next storm?
- I used to find my worth in being a "girl boss," but then I reminded myself that I was God's child before I was ever a girl boss. Does this go against what society pushes on women? How can we remind ourselves we are first His children?
- When was a time your "house" came crumbling down because of a storm? How did you rebuild?

24

WHEN LIFE'S NOT GOING OUR WAY

"I'm so tired of dating!"

Those words came out of my mouth last fall, and they were accompanied by an eye roll as dramatic as a contestant on *The Bachelorette*. Except I *was* the bachelorette, with no hope of anyone accepting my rose. And, yes, I was over it!

I was over trying to date dumb boys. I was tired of dating. I was tired of putting myself out there over and over again only for it not to work out. Also, I was kind of hurt.

I wish I could say I made this remark to a best friend whom I'd known for years. Or on a phone call to my mom. I really wish I could say I stated that to Taylor Swift, receiving dating advice from the queen herself who has helped me through every heartbreak. Nope. I said this to a stranger I had been talking to for all of about two minutes.

Leslie had scheduled an event in her small Texas town, where I was speaking that weekend. My only communication with Leslie before she picked me up at the airport was an Instagram direct message and a few text messages. Now, I don't recommend flying across the country to be picked up by a stranger. But if you do, I hope it is a Leslie.

Leslie listened to me complain about my dating life for the whole hour's drive to her house. I had just been ditched by a great guy. This guy was very intentional for the time we were "talking."

"Talking" is the name millennials and Gen Z'ers created for the phase that comes right before a couple is officially dating. I hate this phase because it can last anywhere from one week to indefinitely. (Scary, right?) When you're stuck in the talking phase with someone, you aren't technically dating, so you aren't exclusive. However, you are catching feelings, hanging out, and getting to know each other.

I wasn't dating this guy officially, but he hinted that was coming as we went on dates. We got to know each other casually for about two months, and it was going well.

Then something changed. Perhaps I bored him. Or maybe he found someone new. The answer is probably both. The most frustrating part for a control freak like me was that I had no closure. When we stopped "talking," he explained that he liked me, but he just got busy. He would never admit this, I'm sure, but if a guy is too busy for you, that really means he doesn't like you *enough*.

As I vented to Leslie during our drive, she did something amazing: she listened. She patiently allowed me to be frustrated with guys. She encouraged me and shared some of her own dating woes. Then she ended by saying something simple but profound: "You've just gotta have hope."

The night before I spoke to Leslie's group, I lay in bed and laughed at myself. Here I was, a twenty-three-year-old traveling across the country to talk to women about how loved they are by Jesus and how He is all they need, all while questioning my worth because a guy I wasn't even dating didn't want to keep going out with me. I thought about what Leslie had told me: "Have hope." The truth was, I didn't have hope that I would ever find a good guy who liked me. I didn't have hope that God was doing good things in my life. I didn't have hope because I stored up lies in my head.

The lies I heard were:

I will never find anyone who wants to stay in my life.

I am not attractive enough for any guy.

Every guy will always find someone better than me.

I need to find love in a human in order to find my purpose. (Big lie!)

And the most toxic one: *If I were writing my story, it would be better than this.*

I think we all have lies we believe. Believing the lies is even more tempting when we become overwhelmed. When disappointment enters our hearts, we are steered away from trusting God. We doubt whether God is for us, whether God is good, and whether God truly knows what He is doing. And those lies don't allow us to live in the hope we've received through Jesus.

God is molding your story beautifully. It does not matter if you're single, married, divorced, or still mourning a guy you were "talking" to . . . God is at work. Your purpose is not dependent on your relationship status. God needs you. A you who is not entangled with doubt about your worth because life is not going your way.

A Healthy Response When Life Doesn't Go Our Way

If we are going to trust that God knows what He's doing, we must live out Psalm 13:

> How long, LORD? Will you forget me forever?
>> How long will you hide your face from me?
> How long must I wrestle with my thoughts

and day after day have sorrow in my heart?
How long will my enemy triumph over me?

Look on me and answer, LORD my God.
Give light to my eyes, or I will sleep in death,
and my enemy will say, "I have overcome him,"
and my foes will rejoice when I fall.

But I trust in your unfailing love;
my heart rejoices in your salvation.
I will sing the LORD's praise,
for he has been good to me.

Psalm 13:1–6

I think this psalm models a healthy way for us to respond when life doesn't go our way. In verses 1–2, David was being honest about his feelings. He had believed the lie that God had forgotten him. He admitted to believing the lie that God was hiding from him.

Then in verses 2–4, David realized that Satan was the one who had been lying to him. When David let himself believe that God was forgetting him, he was allowing the Enemy to triumph over God's truth. So he asked God to answer and reveal Himself in his life.

Finally, in verses 5–6, David trusted that God's love was greater than his present struggle. He realized that salvation was worthy of celebrating in any circumstances. In the end, David even sang praise to God and trusted that the Lord had been good to him.

To summarize David's response:

1. He was honest.
2. He was direct because he knew the Enemy was the source of his woes.
3. He sang praises to God.

On days when your heart breaks—when you are denied the job you interviewed for, your husband says something that hurts you, the boy who took you on some dates ghosts you, or an old friend stabs you in the back—you must have trust and hope.

How to Gain Trust and Hope

When life doesn't turn out the way we expected, we can rant to our moms, and we can rant to strangers like Leslie. We can tell God that it feels like He forgot about us. But when we admit we are struggling with lies, we can allow trust and hope to come into our hearts so that we can sing truth. We have to trust that God knows what He is doing and have hope that there are better days ahead because God is working for our good. Every bad day will lead to a good day, and every rejection is simply protection.

Let's think about how we would do this in our lives.

1. Understand the importance of being honest.

If you aren't honest about the condition of your heart, how can Jesus enter your heart? There is no room for true trust in your heart when it is filled with pride. Be honest about the struggle you are facing. Be honest about your doubts. But when you do face your doubts, instead of running to alcohol, that one past relationship that made you feel wanted, frustration, or even breakup songs, run to Jesus. Be honest with Him.

I see many women—myself included—who feel the pressure to be the "chill girl." We want to be laid-back, emotionless, and known as someone who doesn't question her life after one rejection. This game of pretending is unhealthy. While we're focusing on pretending to be chill, we are suppressing our true emotions. And while we are suppressing our emotions, the Enemy is making his bed in our thoughts.

It is okay to cry. It is okay to doubt. It is okay to be upset. Jesus knows we will do those things, and He said it is truth that sets us free (John 8:32). The first step in learning to trust God is being honest about how far away from Him your thoughts are.

2. Be direct and know who the problem is.

I used to cry in bathrooms after heartbreaks. I was hiding my emotions but also standing in front of the mirror wondering and assuming that the problem always came from the reflection in the mirror. I would analyze how I handled the situation and blame myself, my deepest insecurities, and who I believed myself to be.

If you are ready to trust God, you have to be ready to know who is the source of all your doubts, insecurities, and struggles. It's not your ex, the guy who ghosted you, or the girl who was mean to you. The Bible tells us that our true enemy is Satan.

Trusting God means turning away from who is distracting you from the Lord's goodness. The reason you are doubting your worth is because you're giving in to the Enemy's lies. The reason you are doubting God's goodness is because the Enemy is distracting you from truth.

If you want to win the battle, you must be willing to fight the correct opponent—and that's not the guy who broke your heart. The correct opponent is the one who causes you to doubt yourself, doubt God, and struggle to find peace in your confusion. The opponent is a force only God can defeat. Know your opponent, and pick God to be on your team.

3. Worship is more than a song, so sing a life that thanks God—even in the worst circumstances.

On the tough days, get up, pray, and then go live a life that sings thankfulness to God. Sit and cry if you need to, but don't allow yourself to succumb to a pity party. God is doing something new in your life. God has your back. And if you want to trust Him, begin through worship.

Worship is more than a song. We also worship God by loving a stranger, sharing our hearts with younger friends, and living a life that chooses trust over understanding. You don't need to know all the answers to walk with Jesus—you just need faith. Worship can be done at church with a beautiful band, but it can also be done in a car ride with a friend, in your dorm with your girls, in your cubicle at work, at Waffle House at 1:00 a.m., or, yes, even on the dance floor at weddings. Worship reminds us that God is in the work of doing, and it is our job to be in the work of praising. We praise Him not because life is great, but because we trust that even in the midst of hurt, He is making a way. I hope on your next hard day you choose Jesus anyway. Choose worship. Choose trust. Choose to say, "Life may not be going the way I want, but I trust God."

Talks like the one I had with Leslie are healthy. But I wouldn't recommend revealing those feelings to a stranger. You should confess your feelings and emotions to someone you trust. Someone who will listen. And someone who will remind you there are better days ahead and that God is more powerful than any rejection. Honesty is important because truth can't enter your heart if you're lying about the condition of your heart.

I see many women who do the first part correctly. It's easy to scream at God and complain about the way life is going. But if you allow your story to end at that verse, you will be tired. You will be annoyed. And you will miss out on the true peace and joy that comes with worship.

"You've Just Gotta Have Hope"

I know life isn't going your way. Maybe you wish your dating life was going better. Maybe you wish your marriage was stronger. Yes, you're hurt. Yes, life sucks. But guess what? God's got you. He has you where you are for a reason, and He knows what He is doing. Sing trust on days when you're overwhelmed, and allow Him to write your story.

Please remember that there's no sin in crying. Cry about that test. Cry about your pain. Cry about the disease, your frustration, your mistake, your friend, or the boy you weren't even dating. But as you're crying, fall at the feet of Jesus. Trust that any rejection from this world is simply God's protection. Trust that even when you have no idea what God is doing, He is still there and working for your good.

Don't just know this truth—sing this truth even on your bad days. And remember Leslie's advice: "You've just gotta have hope."

Real Talk

- Is it difficult for you to have hope? Why or why not?
- Read Psalm 13 again. Which is the most difficult for you when you talk to God: being honest, being direct, or singing praises?
- It is not a sin to cry. Do you tend to hide your frustrations and emotions? Why?
- Write an honest prayer to God in which you are direct, and then sing praises to Him at the end. Don't make this prayer short—make it long.

25

WHEN WE'RE NOT SURE WHERE WE'RE GOING

Remember in high school when people asked you, "Where do you see yourself in five years?" As a senior, I said I dreamed of working in public relations for a sports team. I thought I would be engaged, or at least seriously dating someone. I remember looking at my friend Chloe and saying, "One day soon, I'll have the life I want."

As I write this book, I am six years removed from high school. My life after high school sure looks a lot different from what I expected!

I was living paycheck to paycheck. I didn't have a serious boyfriend or even an interest at that time. Or maybe I was upset about some boy I wasn't even dating. Ah, details. But basically, my life was way different from the life I'd dreamed of.

Living in my everyday life is one of my biggest struggles. I get tired of my everyday life. I would prefer my "one-day" life. Life sometimes feels like a ladder, and I am constantly overworking myself only to have to keep climbing.

In high school, I climbed my ladder and couldn't wait for college. Don't get me wrong, I cried some tears and said my good-byes. But then I ran away and didn't look back for a long time. In some ways, that's healthy. But I didn't look back on high school because I idolized the next stage. Finally, my "one day in college" had arrived.

Then I started college and began climbing a new ladder.

I'll never forget that feeling of having achieved a lifelong goal when I graduated college. I had finished that ladder. But with my degree in my hand, I still wanted more. I dreamed of my new one-day life. I wanted financial stability, to own a home, a serious boyfriend or husband, maybe even two cute kids who played soccer.

As I dreamed of my new one-day life, I realized I have never truly enjoyed my life. But the truth was that I needed to embrace my life. I needed to embrace my present. My present is not a reminder of how good my life is; it's a reminder of how good my God is.

God Places Us Where We Need to Be

The story of Esther inspires me to embrace God's sovereignty. Esther's story is told in the Bible book that bears her name.

Esther married a king. In her time, queens did not speak on matters of the kingdom. While she was married to the king, someone tried to kill all Jewish residents in her area. Esther also was Jewish, and she had two options for responding: she could remain silent and safe, or she could stand up for her faith and risk her life to save her fellow believers.

Mordecai, Esther's cousin who had raised her as a daughter after her parents died, suggested to Esther that perhaps she was placed in her position "for such a time as this" (Esther 4:14). Esther decided to stand up for her faith, and her courageous actions eventually saved all the Jews in her area.

I used to read this book of the Bible and think the main point was to compliment Esther's boldness. I made Esther the hero of the story. I think Esther's boldness is something we should all embody, but the older I get, the more I realize that this book actually casts God as the hero.

God places us right where we need to be.

God gives us everything and everyone we need to bring Him glory.

God gives us an opportunity to live a unique purpose and stand up for our faith.

Nothing is by chance with God.

It's easy to dread each day in our current season. Sometimes we feel like middle schoolers, waking up to our annoying alarm, dreading the start of a new day. We feel awkward and out of place. We question our purpose. We ask, *Why am I where I am?*

I cannot tell you why you are where you are at this moment, but I can promise you that it is for a purpose. God is sovereign. He knows what He is doing. God knows what He is doing with you. And God wants to use you.

God Knows What He Is Doing

I regret a lot about my senior year of college. I focused on my future. I worked my butt off and prepared for my first book to be published. I began speaking at churches around the nation. But I forgot to live my current life. I forgot that I was called to live first and prepare second.

My college friends called me out my senior year. I spent too many nights traveling to speak and worrying about my social media and future career. I stopped embracing the platform I had in college. Finally, my best friend, Lauren, convicted me with these words: "Grace, we know you're busy and have a lot in store for your future. But what is God doing in your life right now? If you think He's powerful enough to use you in your 'one day,' why can't He use you in your today?"

Let's all agree that God knows what He is doing. Trust in these three things:

1. God knows what He is doing, and He wants to use you.
2. Every position, title, friend, classmate, and random stranger you meet at the coffee shop is an opportunity God has given you to live for Him. Don't waste your chances.
3. Life is meant to be lived. Stop dreaming about your one-day life and start living in your present. God desires to use you where you are.

I pray that you create a life you love. I hope you plan right, dream big, and prepare when needed for the future. But I pray you also are reminded that you serve a God who brought you to where you are for a reason. There is life to be lived today. Stop striving to find your "one day" and start walking in purpose today.

Let's go back to Esther for another important part of the story. Although Mordecai said Esther might have been brought to the kingdom "for such a time as this" (Esther 4:14), he also said in that same verse that even if Esther did not stand up for God's people, God would save them in His time.

Esther was courageous, but she wasn't the hero. God was the hero.

You aren't the hero. You don't have to be the hero. God wants to use you, but He doesn't have to. God will win. God will pave a way. If you don't choose to be used by Him, He might give the opportunity to others. But you can make it happen today.

How lucky are we to serve a God who desires to use our messy hearts to serve His greater purpose? I hope my everyday life will make God smile. I hope He is happy that He gave feet to someone who walks in purpose and eyes to someone who is alert to His opportunities.

Trusting God means trusting that He is powerful enough to use you today. Live your life. Live your purpose. Let go of your one-day life—and start living today.

Real Talk

- What does your one-day life look like? What is something you are currently working for?
- Read the book of Esther this week. What are two seemingly random coincidences that led to Esther being in the right place at the right time? What does this tell you about God?
- Do you struggle to trust that you are where you are for a reason?
- Do you dread your today? What can you do to find joy and purpose in your today?

CONCLUSION

Read This When You Feel
Like It's Just You

You have finished this book. Congratulations!

I do not know where you read this book. Maybe you read it in a college dorm room or while your children napped in your apartment. Maybe you read this book on the beach or during many lunch breaks at your job. Maybe you read it with a group of friends, or maybe you were alone. I don't care where you read this book or with whom . . . I just hope that as you flip through the last pages you can realize this:

You are not alone.

Don't get me wrong—I hope you view me as your friend and reflect on this book, smiling and saying, "I'm not alone; Grace gets me!" Selfishly, yes, I hope for that. It is cooler for me to think I'm your friend who can bond with you over mistakes, hurts, doubts, and fears. That is way cooler than being just a random writer miles away from you, so let's pretend we are best friends.

I want you to think I am the kind of friend who would hold your hair up if you had too many margaritas but also the kind of friend who would remind you of truth the next day. I want to be the friend who calls you up and helps you see that your purpose is bigger than your struggle today. I hope you realize that life is better when we are honest with ourselves and others. I hope you realize you are not the only one struggling and you truly understand that it is okay to not always be okay. You do not always have to be the strong one. You aren't alone, and there are people in your life who are struggling too. I'm one of them, but chances are, your friends are experiencing hurt and disappointment as well. And they don't need the "fake it till I make it" you. They need the real you. They need to know they aren't alone.

So, yes, you aren't alone in your struggle. I get you, and your friends probably understand how you feel. We are all more alike than we think.

But you also aren't alone because you have a Savior in front of you.

A Savior who wants the real you and wants you to step toward your purpose.

So what *is* the purpose of all this?

I've noticed in my life that the reason I forget what I'm created for is because I'm not looking at my Creator.

Let me say that again another way: when you stop looking at your Creator, you forget what you were created for.

When you stop looking at the One who gave you life, you forget what life is about.

When you settle for loneliness instead of looking at the One who cares for you, you forget how far God has brought you.

You aren't alone because your Savior goes before you. He went before you and endured the cross for you. And now in the midst of it all, He stands on top of the storm and asks you to walk toward Him. He's asking you to trust Him. Now the choice is yours.

Keep Your Eyes on Jesus

Peter was one of the men in the Bible who was closest to Jesus. He followed Jesus while He walked the earth, and Peter even walked on water with Jesus. It happened in the midst of a storm. We've already talked about the disciples thinking Jesus was a ghost, but let's dig in more. Matthew 14:22–33 tells us the rest of the story.

> Immediately Jesus made the disciples get into the boat and go on ahead of him to the other side, while he dismissed the crowd. After he had dismissed them, he went up on a mountainside by himself to pray. Later that night, he was there alone, and the boat was already a considerable distance from land, buffeted by the waves because the wind was against it.
>
> Shortly before dawn Jesus went out to them, walking on the lake. When the disciples saw him walking on the lake, they were terrified. "It's a ghost," they said, and cried out in fear.
>
> But Jesus immediately said to them: "Take courage! It is I. Don't be afraid."
>
> "Lord, if it's you," Peter replied, "tell me to come to you on the water."
>
> "Come," he said.
>
> Then Peter got down out of the boat, walked on the water and came toward Jesus. But when he saw the wind, he was afraid and, beginning to sink, cried out, "Lord, save me!"
>
> Immediately Jesus reached out his hand and caught him. "You of little faith," he said, "why did you doubt?"

And when they climbed into the boat, the wind died down. Then those who were in the boat worshiped him, saying, "Truly you are the Son of God."

Jesus was walking on water. Peter saw Jesus and asked for Jesus to call out to him. Then Peter started strutting his stuff on top of the water.

Peter, a regular human being like you and me, was walking on water as he kept his eyes on Jesus. Everything was going great. But then Peter noticed the wind whipping around him and began to sink.

I read this story again recently and laughed. Here I am, in the midst of my busyness, doubts, and loneliness, out here trying to find my purpose, and you know what? I do great sometimes. When I look at Jesus, I can find strength, adventure, and joy. I walk on water for a hot second. When I look at Jesus, I can do the unthinkable. But the minute I look at the winds—my busy schedule, what others think about me, or the question, "Is it just me?"—I start to sink. I sink not because the wind is stronger than Jesus, but because I lose sight of my Savior. I thought I was alone and forgot to notice my Savior in front of me saying, "Come."

"But when Grace found her worth in her schedule, she began to sink."

"But when Grace thought her everyday was about her, she began to sink."

"But when Grace cared more about what other people thought of her than what Jesus thinks, she began to sink."

"But when Grace cared more about someone's opinion than her Creator, she began to sink."

"But when Grace lied and said she was fine, she began to sink."

And like I've said, if you stop looking at the One who gives you life, you'll forget what life is all about.

See, the world tells you it is smart to look at the storm. You're being sensible. You are being careful. You are being realistic. I mean, the storm is strong, and you should be cautious and keep your eye on the obstacles . . . right?

Well, I can promise you that when you do what Peter did and look at the storm, you are choosing caution over trust. You are choosing the realistic over the holy. And you are choosing loneliness over a relationship with your Savior.

This passage never once denied the strength of the winds. In fact, in the beginning the writer made sure to tell us the storm was strong. The winds were rocking the boat. But even when the storm rocked their boat, their Savior stood strong. Was He a clear figure that was obvious to see? No. But He was there. And you are like Peter, with two important choices:

1. *Will you step out of the boat?* Will you go against what those around you are doing? Will you choose being known over the comfort of "normal"?
2. *Will you keep your eyes on Jesus?* Will you do something big because you're looking at your big Savior? Even when the winds are strong, will you trust that your Savior is stronger? Will you look toward Him?

To my lonely, baggy-eyed, frustrated friend: breathe in, breathe out. You are not alone. You have a Savior in front of you. Take one step forward. Keep your eyes on Jesus. Yes, the wind is strong, but Jesus is stronger. Yes, your schedule is busy, but Jesus is greater. Yes, there is a storm swirling around you, but Jesus desires to show you His power in the storm.

So often I want Jesus to just end the storm. I mean, wouldn't that be nice? Couldn't He just end my financial problems and crappy situations? And the truth is that, yes, He could. But when I read the story about Jesus and Peter walking on water in the midst of the storm,

I'm impressed. I see the beauty that comes from a God greater than the storm.

So if you're wondering why there is a storm, maybe it is because Jesus is creating an opportunity for you to be bold. Maybe the storm is simply a tool given to you by the One who can and will calm that storm.

And in the end of this passage in the Bible, all the disciples worshipped Jesus. See, Peter's boldness and Jesus' sovereignty inspired more people than just Peter. Peter's slipup taught them all a great lesson. When Peter looked at the winds and began to sink, he still cried out, "Lord, save me." He didn't try to dog-paddle and fix it himself. He didn't pretend to have it all together. He called out for help. And the disciples all worshipped Jesus when Peter and Jesus got back in the boat. Peter wasn't worshipped, even though he, too, walked on water. Jesus was worshipped because Peter's experience pointed to his Savior, and Peter's slipup was used to show Jesus' sovereignty.

Peter's relationship with Jesus, the good moments and the doubtful moments, all showed others how great it is to trust in Jesus. This is the life we want to live. One that inspires others to worship Jesus when we return. Did Peter do something cool and walk on water? Yes. But he pointed to Jesus and others worshipped Jesus because of this.

You Aren't the Only One

Throughout this book we've come again and again to the point that you aren't alone. But the fact is, even if you don't feel alone now, you probably will again. That's why I want to leave you with some final reminders for when that time inevitably comes. On the days when you are struggling and think it's just you, I hope you respond to your questions like this:

1. Am I the only one who is tired, overwhelmed, doubting, and fearful?

No, you aren't the only one. There is a storm around you and a boat full of people out here scared, doubtful, hurt, and worried. But there's also a Savior in front of you. Life is overwhelming, and the storm will rock you. But are you going to live a life that leaves behind what the world considers normal? My prayer is that you'll be like Peter and you would rather be one step closer to Jesus than "safe" on a boat hiding from your purpose. Jesus is working in the midst of your storm. He is there. It might be dark, scary, and windy, but He is there.

2. Am I the only one who feels hurt and lonely?

No, you aren't the only one. But the reason you feel alone is because you are choosing caution over boldness. Step out of your boat, and walk toward truth. You're safer when you walk toward honesty, truth, and your Savior who wants you to come to Him on the hard days. Latch on to your purpose, and trust Him. Stop looking at the winds, stop looking at others' opinions, and walk toward Jesus. Jesus will calm the storm in His perfect timing. Trust that Jesus is working in the background and that His timing is perfect. While you wait for the storm to be calmed, trust Him.

3. Am I the only one who is still searching for my purpose?

No, you aren't the only one. Remember, though, that Jesus has personally invited you to do big things. Jesus wants to give you the opportunity to show the people around you His power. However, if you want to do big things, look toward your big Savior. Purpose is not about hustle or becoming a girl boss. Purpose is about walking toward the One who saved you. Jesus gives you purpose. Your purpose isn't to wish away the storm. Your purpose is to embrace Him and show boldness even in the midst of your storm. Trust Him even when your life is a storm.

4. Am I the only one struggling to trust that God is —— there?

No, you aren't the only one. But faith has nothing to do with what makes sense; it has everything to do with your boldness. Faith requires boldness, not answers. So walk toward Jesus, and when you stray and look at the winds and feel like you're sinking, say, "Lord, save me!" Call out to Him, and He will answer.

5. Am I the only one confused about how to be an —— adult?

No, you aren't the only one. Your purpose isn't financial stability, a successful career, or a strong social life. Your life is a gift, so thank the Giver. The Giver who gives you His peace and love every day. The Giver who wants you to look at Him. The Giver whom you have the ability to look toward in the midst of your busy life.

Step into Your Purpose

I pray that you live a life that is adventurous. I pray that you look toward Jesus and live in the truth that He is always at work. I pray you remember that in order to soar on wings like eagles on the days that overwhelm you, you have to trust in Him.

Trust must be chosen daily. Live in trust, and walk in your purpose. It won't always be easy, and trust can sometimes make life more confusing. But trusting in your Creator leads you to find what you were created for. And when you walk in this purpose, you will realize you aren't alone. So as you close this book, step into your purpose by stepping toward Jesus. The adventure begins when you realize you can truly trust in Him.

Real Talk

- How will you respond the next time you feel alone?
- How can you help others not feel alone?
- How can you remind yourself that you have a Savior in front of you?
- What can you do to look toward Jesus more in your storms?
- Write a prayer to God. Ask Him to lead you to purpose.

FORTY TRUTHS WHEN YOU FEEL ALONE

We have talked about our weariness, hurts, and tension, but most importantly, the freedom that comes from chasing Jesus and trusting in Him. We have learned that Jesus gives us eagerness, patience, and adventure, but settling for loneliness over true relationships only leaves us feeling empty. We have talked about it all. But the real work that comes from the growth process we are in does not come from reading. It comes from living. It comes from deciding to grow in His name. It comes from your tomorrow and the way you pursue His strength by trusting in Him.

I wish I could hang out and talk to you forever, but you have big things ahead. You have a life to be lived and purpose to carry out. But before we wrap up this book and you step out into your new adventure, I want to leave with you these truths for when you feel alone. The next time you feel overwhelmed, annoyed, or defeated, I pray that you return to this book to read these forty truths.

1. You can't always be liked. But you can always pray. On the day others' opinions seem loud, create quiet time with Jesus and pray.

2. You can't control your circumstances, but you can control your thoughts. Make your thoughts meaningful.

3. On your difficult days, eat ice cream.

4. On your difficult days, call an old friend.

5. Call your mom or grandmother or a trusted older friend. You can google for some answers, but you can't google wisdom.

6. Saying no is not a bad thing.

7. Saying yes is not required.

8. Succeeding isn't required either. You are not required to succeed every time. You will not always win. But you can always choose to be kind.

9. Someone else's success does not mean that you lack success. Stop comparing how a squirrel and a monkey climb a tree. They climb by different means and at different speeds—because they are different. You and your peers are different too.

10. Celebrate your differences. You are not her, and you are not him. That is not a bad thing. This just shows how unique your God is.

11. You'll never regret living out love.

12. You'll never regret not going off at the manager who annoyed you. (This one is personal, okay?)

13. Gentle words are powerful, but so are hurtful words. Choose to be gentle even when you are annoyed.

14. When someone annoys you, control what you can control. You can't control that person, but you can control your thoughts. Pray for patient thoughts. Hurt people hurt people. Lonely people try to make others feel alone. Remember you aren't alone, and live a life that reminds even those who hurt you that you aren't alone.

15. Frustration can either be just or sinful. Frustration is not always bad. Pray for wisdom to decipher the difference.

16. Life is too short to waste your hours or days proving yourself to others. Pursue Jesus, not approval.

17. If someone rejects you, move on.

18. Just because you have been treated like crap does not mean you are not worthy. Do not settle for less than you deserve.

19. Christians will sometimes suck. You will be hurt by them. But you will never be hurt by Jesus.

20. Thank Jesus that He still loves you even when you sometimes suck.

21. Christianity is only boring if you make it boring. Live life with adventure, not fear.

22. When fear controls your tomorrow, trust gives you the strength to live in your today.

23. For my single ladies: if he doesn't text you back, move on. And remember that purpose is not dependent on your relationship status. Singleness is beautiful.

24. For my taken ladies: pursue Jesus together as a couple. You'll grow tired of each other if you don't look toward Jesus as a foundation for your relationship.

25. You will never regret obeying Jesus.

26. You will regret taking shots. Trust me.

27. If you're using Scripture to condone what you know is wrong, you are reading Scripture wrong.

28. Stop labeling people by their past and start labeling people by their Savior.

29. Reputations aren't going to be read in eternity.

30. Get back on your bike.

31. Trust again.

32. Pray about it again.

33. Never let the fear of failing stop you from living in your calling. God doesn't call you to success; He calls you to purpose.

34. Isaiah 40:30 says, "Even youths will become weak and tired, and young men will fall in exhaustion" (NLT). We will all be tired at some point. We will all become frustrated and stumble into lonely days. We will all fail at some point. It's normal.

35. Isaiah 40:31 says, "Those who hope in the LORD will renew their strength." If you want to be strong, you have to go to the One who is always strong. Only the Lord can give you strength when you are tired or have failed.

36. The gospel is more important than your opinion. Let truth be louder than your opinion.

37. Speak the Spirit, not your mind.

38. Patience can't be faked. Patience requires a pure heart.

39. Faking it till you make it is impossible. If you fake it, you will not make it. If you are in a storm, admit it.

40. Live for Jesus and not just for eternity with Him. Live for Jesus so you get a life with Him starting today.

I pray that your days are filled with more laughter and fewer tears. I pray that you live a life that makes you smile and feel thankful to be alive. I pray that on the days when you struggle, you will ask Him to renew your strength. I pray that on the lonely days you will trust Jesus. I pray that you realize trust is not a destination but a verb you will act on daily.

God wants to use you. He wants the baggy-eyed, tired you. The you that is running on coffee and disappointment. He wants the overwhelmed you. God desires to renew your strength. He desires for you to release your busyness and weariness and finally begin to truly trust Him. Release your tension, and take that step toward Him.

Real Talk

- Which points resonated with you the most?
- Write down the most meaningful of these points, and read them daily. Where can you place these reminders?
- Write a prayer for your tomorrow. How do you want to pursue God? How will you live a life that trusts in Him? How will you find your strength in Him? Ask God to grant you wisdom.

ACKNOWLEDGMENTS

If you read my book, you've probably realized I am sometimes obnoxious and always dramatic. I know what you're thinking . . . *No, Grace, don't talk down about yourself; God created you beautifully!*

God makes no mistakes, and I know that . . . but when He created me, I think He laughed a little. He knew I would be one hot mess—an overachiever, overthinker, loud talker, and big dreamer—and I am so thankful He made me this way. However, I also know that when He created my people, He knew He had to give me people who were patient, encouraging, and cheerleaders for the kingdom. People who would remind me on the hard days to chase my purpose, chase my Jesus, and lower my voice (in a nice way, of course!). So as I reflect and desire to acknowledge the people who made this book and the past couple years so sweet, I can't help but first thank God. Thank You, God, for giving women opportunities my grandma never saw. Thank You for giving me people who love me well. Thank You for giving me Your Son, who died for me, so I can live for You and live with others in Your name.

To my family . . . the book is dedicated to y'all for a reason. We are all so different, but I truly learned this year that you all have my back.

To my father . . . thank you for always believing in my dreams, and also thanks for doing my taxes. You push me to be my best and love me despite my flaws.

To my mother . . . we are very different but also very similar. I love you for that. Thank you for loving me.

To my brother . . . no one hates social media more than you! Thank you for making fun of me and keeping me humble. I am thankful we are complete opposites and you always show me a different opinion. Thank you for allowing me to follow you to Baylor, and thank you for always supporting me.

To my grandmother Valentine (Maw-Maw). I think we are more alike than we even realize. Thank you for being my biggest fan. Happy eightieth birthday! I am better, louder, stronger, and more optimistic because of you.

To my grandmother Herbert . . . growing up I remember you coming to our house and sitting in the rocking chair reading books. It makes me so happy to know you now can read my books. Thank you for the support always.

To my hometown friends . . . especially Chloe and Paige. I'm so glad I still have y'all. Miles may separate us, but I'm thankful you are both a FaceTime away.

To my first church and first pastor . . . Rev. James, I am so thankful for what I learned from growing up in your pews. I am thankful for the way you lead St. Timothy UMC and for your beautiful wife, Delaine.

To my teachers growing up . . . especially Mrs. Benton, Mrs. Tully, Mrs. Easterling, Mrs. Rhodus, Mrs. Dendinger, Mrs. Jarrell, Mrs. Parker, Mr. Delouche, Mrs. Sisney, and so many more. I am thankful to have had teachers who loved me and reminded me that I should always be a learner. And I'm especially thankful for my English teachers' red pens! They prepared me for this career.

To the greatest principal ever . . . Johnny V. Thank you for holding our school to high standards and pushing me to be my best. I still owe you for allowing me to take that selfie at graduation!

To all my college professors . . . but especially the Baylor journalism department. Thank you for pushing me and believing in me. I am smarter, wiser, and a dreamer because of my professors.

To my college best friends . . . Britta, Nora, Lauren, Dresden, Ariah, Emma, Sam, and so many more. I am better because of you all. Thanks for listening to my dreams more than anyone I know. Thank you for believing in me.

To my Orlando "moms" . . . Kathy, Adair, Candace, Angie, Barbie, and so many more. Thank you for always supporting me through different seasons. I hope to love the next young Orlando-transplant when I'm older.

To the other women in Orlando who support me . . . Lisa, Kimberly, Corrine, Michelle, Kelly, and so many more. I am thankful to know y'all are a phone call (and street) away. Thank you for loving me well.

To two families who have opened up their families and homes to me in Orlando . . . the Houstons and Demers. Thank you for loving me, for letting me hang out with your fun and beautiful children, and for giving me a job when I needed one!

To Catherine, Seth, Stergy, and Sadie de Armas. Thank you for being a second family. Catherine, I will forever be thankful for you. You are truly my big sister.

To my Orlando community . . . the friends who make lunch fun and walks a social event . . . I am so thankful. I can't list everyone, but I want to especially thank McKenzie, Lizzy, Kristi, Caroline, Kettley, Brooke R., Emma K., Brooke G., Kristin, Lindsey, Kenzie, Catherine, and so many more. Thank you for being good friends.

To Crestridge . . . thank you for giving me a safe and adventurous place to grow in faith as a young girl. And thank you for a job that brought me lifelong friendships. Haylee, Sarah B., Sarah S., Anna Mahr, Kelsey, Meredith G., Madeline G., Sophie, Amber, Mckenzie, Robyn, and so many more . . . I am thankful I have y'all by my side.

To Beth Moore, thank you for teaching me to be bold in my calling and to love God's Word.

And to Taylor Swift, please notice me, haha! I am a lover of words because of you, and I still have hope I can meet you in person one day.

And to every reader, thank you. Thank you for listening to me. I hope to continue to write more books and open up my life to you. I hope to meet every one of you one day somehow. And may the Lord find my words faithful to Him.

—xoxo,
Grace Valentine

ABOUT THE AUTHOR

Grace Valentine is an author, blogger, podcast host, and speaker. Her readers love the fact that she is young, ordinary, and relatable; they say her fresh voice helps them navigate their own faith and life. Grace's mission is to show others that Christianity is not lame—it is an adventure worth living.

Grace grew up right by New Orleans, Louisiana, in a suburban town called Mandeville. She graduated from Baylor University in 2018 with a degree in journalism. She currently resides in Orlando, Florida, where she enjoys going on runs and eating lots of sushi. You can find Grace on Instagram @thegracevalentine; her podcast, *I'm Tired*; Twitter @GraceV96; or her website, www.gracevalentine.org. Grace loves connecting with her readers, so send her a message!